D1645893

NOT JUST TOBACCO:

HEALTH SCARES, MEDICAL PATERNALISM AND INDIVIDUAL LIBERTY

CHRIS R. TAME

WITH A PREFACE BY SEAN GABB

THE HAMPDEN PRESS
DEAL
MMXVI

Not Just Tobacco:
Health Scares, Medical Paternalism and Individual Liberty,
by Chris R. Tame
© Chris R. Tame, Sean Gabb, 2016

First Print Edition: November 2016

ISBN-13: 978-1537250496
ISBN-10: 1537250493

Published by:
The Hampden Press
73 Middle Street
Deal
Kent CT14 6HN
England
Telephone: 07956 472 199
sean@seangabb.co.uk
www.seangabb.co.uk

Contents

Preface by Sean Gabb (2016)

The Freedom Organisation for the Right to Enjoy Smoking Tobacco (FOREST) was an organisation set up in 1979 by the British tobacco industry for the purpose described in its name. Its first Directors were Air Chief Marshal Sir Christopher Foxley-Norris and Lieutenant-General Sir Geoffrey Charles Evans. Though men of some distinction, neither had experience of dealing with the corporate bureaucrats who funded their activities. Their names remained on the headed notepaper, but they were replaced in 1981 by Stephen Eyres, who had been an effective Campaigns Director at the Freedom Association. Under his leadership, FOREST settled into a well-funded and well-connected opposition to the growing clamour against the tobacco industry and its customers. His genius lay in persuading his funders that his increasingly libertarian campaign for free choice was no danger to their own wish for a compromise with the prohibitionists.

His weakness was a great and undiscriminating taste for the company of strangers. Late in 1987, he began to show the symptoms of an illness he had done nothing to avoid. By the following summer, he was incapable of managing the daily affairs of FOREST, and he appointed Chris Tame as the Campaigns Director.

Chris took on the position with much enthusiasm. He had already distinguished himself as Manager of the Alternative Bookshop in Covent Garden, and as Director of the Libertarian Alliance. He had been considering a position in the Institute of Economic Affairs, or in some other organisation that focussed on economics. The offer from Eyres seemed far better. Unlike most other libertarians and conservatives in the 1980s, Chris no longer saw traditional socialism as the main enemy. The Soviet Union was a power in evident decline. State socialism, as defined by nationalisation for the benefit of the working classes, was equally in decline. The enemies now of our traditional liberties wore business suits and looked like social democrats. They had no interest in nationalisation and little in high income taxes and welfare redistribution. Their road to power lay through the regulation of thought and lifestyle.

Many of his friends thought defending the right to smoke was at best a diversion from the real struggle. Chris saw it as central to the real struggle.

The enemy was not stupid union leaders or ranting Trotskyites. It was a group that goes under many names, but that may for the moment be called the Enemy Class, and that may loosely be defined as those administrators, lawyers, experts, educators and media people whose living is connected with the State, and whose guiding principle is belief in their right and duty to tell everyone else how to live. Such people, of course, have always been with us. What made these people different was their swelling numbers, and their fondness for ideologies of control that made them a collective, though not wholly cohesive, enemy of the English liberal tradition.

Though constrained by a small budget, Chris spent the next year putting detail into a strategy that Eyres had already outlined, but for which he lacked the intellectual resources. This was to give the tobacco industry just enough short term public relations to keep its managers happy, and to make a purely token effort at populist outreach. The main effort was to be a sustained attack on the ideological bases of the Enemy Class. A month or so after taking up his position at FOREST, Chris asked me to write about the theology of free choice as it applied to tobacco. After I had delivered the manuscript, he commissioned me to ghost or edit a series of short books. These took their evidence from the debate on smoking, but they were always an attack on the Enemy Class.

Sadly, by the end of 1989, Eyres reached a crisis in his moral and physical decline. Never very scrupulous in his use of money, he had turned to outright embezzlement. I am not sure how much money he stole from the FOREST accounts, but it was more than £100,000 – money all spent on unlikely therapies, or on paying for enthusiasms that continued until just a few weeks before his death. The discovery of his crimes would always have been a problem for the organisation. The coincidental appointment of Ralph Harris to the governing board of FOREST made it into a problem for Chris.

The appearance Harris gave the world was of an affable pipe-smoker. He wrote well, and he had a way with charming money from tight-fisted businessmen. He was also a man of dark and even villainous passions. If I choose to pass over the more scandalous facts, his many adulteries had opened him to blackmail. Eyres had no inclination to spend his last months in a prison hospital, and he threatened Harris with a letter to *The Guardian*. The deal then worked out was that Chris should be sacked. The police would not be set on him, but the funders would be told that he was at least partly to blame for the vanished money.

This was one of the few Harris plots that failed, and, while Eyres was paid off most generously to console him for blindness and the amputation of his toes, Chris was appointed Director of FOREST in January 1990. He was forty, and in charge of an organisation that he hoped he could use to make a difference. Harris thought otherwise. He never forgave Chris for besting him. If for other reasons, the tobacco people agreed. The Eyres scandal had undermined their willingness to let FOREST go about its work with only loose supervision. Over the next few years, the budget was repeatedly cut. Chris was forced to give up most of his ideological project, putting his time instead into fighting discrimination against smokers in their places of work. Early in 1995, he was *released* from his contract. I attended his leaving party. Harris made a farewell speech of lush praise, and had already put the word round to stop Chris from finding work anywhere else.

The text here republished was written after Chris had left FOREST. His leaving package included some tapering consultancy of which this was one of the last items. He was never a fluent writer, and the failure of his professional hopes, and the gathering disintegration of his marriage, had left him depressed. He asked David Botsford for help. But David was falling into a depression of his own. Work on the book went slowly. A few weeks before the deadline, Chris asked me to help.

Reading the complete text for the first time in twenty years, I can often see my work. There are many passages that I remember having written, and several more that sound like me. But the text is properly described as the work of Chris Tame. He provided both tone and overall structure. Sat at home in Charlton, I would put together the Tame and Botsford fragments, filling out the blanks, until I had a draft of one of the sections. I would e-mail it to Chris as a plaintext. He would print it and write all over it, and provide another half dozen clippings, and post it to David, who would then type it into WordPerfect 5.1, and post me the disk for approval and amendments. We met several times in Central London to discuss the analytical approach we were trying to develop. Our last review meeting was in a coffee bar in Southampton Row. In all but matters of style and grammar, we deferred to Chris. After I had printed and read the consolidated text, I spoke to David on the telephone. We agreed that Chris had overseen the production of something important that would have an impact on the debate over lifestyle regulation.

Harris disagreed. By now, he was in unchallenged control of FOREST, and this was not something he wanted *his* FOREST to publish. I am told his first act when shown the manuscript was to cross out my name – he never much liked me, though why is no longer relevant. This done, he cut half the evidence and neutered the analysis. As I could only bring myself to skim the version that he allowed through the press, I cannot say in detail what was published. But no one thought it very important, and it had no impact.

It is now twenty years later. Harris is dead. So is Chris. So is David. As the only man left who had any share in its production, and since I am taking the trouble to publish it and offer it for sale, I feel obliged to say what I think of the complete version of the text. Do I still think it as good as its three authors did over the coffee cups in Southampton Row? Or has it, after so long, become as dated as some turgid report of its day from the Adam Smith Institute?

I do not think the factual claims we discuss have dated. The mass of news clippings that Chris provided are all a generation old. Almost any one of them could go, without looking out of place, into a newspaper published tomorrow.

Take this:

> "Eating too many pickled onions increases the risk of throat cancer and a preference for taking very hot soup or drinks as well will increase the risk further." (*The Independent*, 29 May 1992)

Or this:

> "Nearly 35,000 children a week drink more alcohol than the safe limit for adults, survey findings show ... as the Drinkwise campaign was launched ... 'It is estimated from this survey that 130,000 children under the age of 16 claim to be drinking alcohol regularly in pubs', the [Health Education Authority] says." (*The Guardian*, 12 June, 1990)

Or this:

> "Frying or barbecuing meat, chicken or fish produces potentially cancer-causing substances [according to the] US National Cancer Institute." (*The Irish Times*, 27 March, 1991)

The claims have not dated. Nor have the responses we made in the text, or referred to in the notes. This gives our work a value none of us imagined in 1996. If someone tells you, with high authority, that the world will end next Tuesday, you may or may not be persuaded. If you learn that he made the same prediction for last Tuesday, and the Tuesday before that, and for any number of other Tuesdays stretching back into the more or less distant past, you will need to be in the grip of some unusual passion not to regard him as insane or a fraud. The *obesity time bomb* has still not exploded. Mad Cow Disease has not yet rotted our minds. The young men of 1996 who were said to be destroying themselves with cheap lager do not seem to be falling dead in middle age. If for no other reason, what we wrote in 1996 is worth reading today for its deflating effect on the latest scare stories.

I am less happy with some of our analysis. We believed that the purpose of the various scares was to lead us into a total state based on health fascism, and that this purpose would be achieved without firm ideological opposition. But there has been no firm ideological opposition. Since we wrote, the British libertarian movement has pretty well died. Before illness claimed him, Eyres was a man of ability. Harris, whatever can be said against him, bordered on greatness, and his peerage was one of Margaret Thatcher's less risible creations. Since 1996, British libertarianism had decayed into an organised mediocrity, enlivened by a set of bizarre personality cults. Yet the continued freshness of the evidence we accumulated falsifies our prediction. Scare stories can only be recycled as they have been when they remain unaddressed.

Undoubtedly, England has become a more authoritarian country than it was in 1996. Speech is less free. The rule of law has been weakened. Another generation of having news and entertainment and education in the grip of the Enemy Class has left an English people still more degraded and hysterical than it was a year before Diana had her car crash. But Mars Bars and bacon remain openly on sale. Coffee is still untaxed and has no statutory warnings all over its packaging. Cigarettes are more expensive than they were, and they can be smoked in fewer places. But the Puritan State we predicted seems, in its full imposition, as distant now as it was then.

Something we failed to predict was how the Enemy Class would behave once it was fully in power. No doubt, it still has members who dream of putting everyone on a diet of raw porridge and boiled potatoes, and are willing to lock anyone away who gives them a funny look. I was once in a radio debate with a health bureaucrat who wanted to deny cigarettes to terminal cancer patients. Her argument was that a hospital was supposed to be *a place of healing*, and that smoking had no place there.

In the main, however, the Enemy Class in power is less like a plague bacillus than a parasite. Its members have salaries and status. If there are many more of them today than in 1996, they are more interested in controlling whatever moves than in stopping it from moving. They want to *educate* us about the dangers of passive drinking. They want *voluntary agreements* on how things can be described and where they can be sold. They want to commission endless further *research* by their friends. With few exceptions, they do not really want to ban anything. I repeat that nearly all the things attacked in 1996 remain openly available.

Another failure was our dismissal of big business. I did not write this passage in the text, but I did agree with it:

> The[…] tendency [of corporate bureaucrats] is to engage in what can only be called pre-emptive cringing. They lean over backwards to be "reasonable." Instead of confronting, refuting and defeating their enemies, they produce platitudes. They have no conception of the nature of the opposition they face from enemies determined to cripple or destroy them. They "compromise" when compromise only encourages their opponents, and opens the door to the next restriction. They rely on PR hacks who have little understanding of the power of political ideologies and no idea how to combat them. They think things can be sorted out with behind-the-scenes "deals" with politicians – who cannot be trusted and will succumb to whosoever exerts the most pressure.

All three of us were feeling bitter about the failure of these people to see our merits and shower us with even half the money Steven Eyres spent on amyl nitrate. Well, they were right. Compromise worked – or it has so far. They bribed. They wheedled. They selectively gave in. They employed Enemy Class consultants and learned how to turn away wrath by learning to speak the language of that class. They recognised the changing nature of that class in power from total state revolutionaries to rent-seeking *apparatchiks*, and made all necessary adaptations. They faced the resulting increase in costs just as they might any increase in their material costs. They even took take advantage of the new order that was ushered fully into being with Tony Blair's first election victory. Advertising bans were made into opportunities for cartelising cost. Regulations were turned into the means of preserving market share against competition from outside.

And that was it. Business went on as usual. Old products were improved, new products introduced. Prices of nearly everything continued to fall in real terms. Better technology aside, we live in a world not radically different from that of 1996. Indeed, the past twenty years seem to me a kind of endless present – the same hysterical preaching of threats and calls to action, the same lack of really decisive action. We may be sinking, but we have not yet broken in half, and the deck chairs have not substantially moved.

I think, even so, we were right in our claim that the function of all these revolving health scares was to make people into a flock of terrified sheep. If we can be alarmed into diets that make Orthodox Judaism look sensible, or if we can be made to believe that too much washing will give us cancer, or that every male over the age of five is a potential paedophile, or that leaving a few lights on will make our planet into a copy of Venus – why, no one will complain about the salaries and pensions lavished on our new masters, or about the generally more authoritarian state we nowadays endure. If we exaggerated the effect of the scares on their formal targets, there is no doubt of how they helped legitimise the emergence of a new and generally more authoritarian ruling class. Revealing the methods used may not in itself undo this legitimisation. But the ammunition it provides remains useful for a broader attack.

Aware, then, of its virtues and its faults, I commend the present text. If it can have any part of the effect its authors hoped it would, I shall not have published in vain.

Sean Gabb
Deal
April 2016

Were the government to prescribe to us our medicine and diet, our bodies would be in such keeping as our souls are now. Thus in France the emetic was once forbidden and the potato as an article of food. Government is just as infallible, too, when it fixes systems in physics. Galileo was sent to the Inquisition for affirming that the earth was a sphere; the government had declared it to be as flat as a trencher, and Galileo was obliged to abjure his error.

Thomas Jefferson, *Notes on the State of Virginia*, Prichard and Hall, Philadelphia, 1788, p. 169

A man may not always eat and drink what is good for him; but it is better for him and less ignominious to die of gout freely than to have a censor officially appointed over his diet, who after all could not render him immortal. So we urge that while we certainly have neither the lights nor the strength of will to act always for the eventual good of all whom our conduct effects, yet it is better that we should blunder freely in love, in politics, and in religion, than that we should follow the prescriptions of external authorities, dubious authorities at best, which might save us a few knocks, only to lead us and the world, in their ponderous blindness, to the most hideous catastrophes.

George Santayana, *Dominations and Powers: Reflections on Liberty, Society and Government*, Charles Scribner's Sons, New York, 1951, p. 184

The maxim, that governments ought to train the people in the way in which they should go, sounds well. But is there any reason for believing that a government is more likely to lead the people in the right way than the people to fall into the right way of themselves? ...

Nothing is so galling to a people, not broken in from the birth, as a paternal, or, in other words, a meddling government, a government which tells them what to read, and say, and eat, and drink, and wear.

Thomas B. Macaulay, "Southey's Colloquies" (1830), *Critical and Historical Essays*, J. M. Dent/Everyman edition, London, 1906, pp. 207, 212

Now what I contend is that my body is my own, at least I have always regarded it. If I do harm through my experimenting with it, it is I who suffer, not the state.

Mark Twain

I'd rather that England should be free than that England should be compulsorily sober. With freedom we might in the end attain sobriety, but in the other alternative we should eventually lose both freedom and sobriety.

W. C. Magee (The Archbishop of York), *Sermon at Peterborough*, 1868

Of all tyrannies a tyranny sincerely exercised for the good of its victims may be the most oppressive. It may be better to live under robber barons than under omnipotent moral busybodies. The robber baron's cruelty may sometimes sleep, his cupidity may at some point be satiated; but those who torment us for our own good will torment us without end, for they do so with the approval of their own consciences ...

Where benevolent planning, armed with political and economic power, becomes wicked is when it tramples on people's rights for the sake of their own good.

C. S. Lewis

Good intention will always be pleaded for every assumption of power ... It is hardly too strong to say that the Constitution was made to guard the people against the dangers of good intentions. There are men in all ages who mean to govern well, but they mean to govern. They promise to be good masters, but they mean to be masters.

Daniel Webster

I: INTRODUCTION

The current war against tobacco should not be seen as an isolated phenomenon. Indeed it cannot be understood fully – or effectively criticised – outside of a much broader context, including those of ethics, political ideology, the nature of special interest groups, class conflict, and the nature of science, amongst others.

In a previous paper, *Non-Smokers Unite: An Appeal to Fellow Non-Smokers, or, Why Non-Smokers Should Support the Rights of Smokers* (1), Chris Tame discussed the role of the anti-smoking movement as a "post-socialist" disguise for statism and bureaucratic power. In this paper we want to place it in the context of the myriad other health scares and paternalist campaigns that seem to monopolise so much of the media's space and attention.

The year 1962 saw the publication of *Les Propagandes*, the definitive study of the role played by propaganda in the exercise of political power in contemporary societies, by Professor Jacques Ellul, of the Institut du Etudes Politiques of Bordeaux. The book is a powerful work of political analysis. Certainly nobody who has read it will look at the way opinions are formed in our society in quite the same way again. In seeking to understand the nature of the endless succession of health scares to which the people of this country are subjected by health pressure groups, some private but more frequently state-supported, and by both the privately-owned and nationalised media, we will first examine Professor Ellul's thesis. In its light we will survey a number of these health scares and examine the fallacies on which they are based. We will outline the lessons to be learned by those concerned for the maintenance of both the quality and integrity of the scientific endeavour, and of the cause of individual liberty and free choice.

II: PROPAGANDA AND THE INDIVIDUAL

Ellul recognises that all propaganda addresses the individual in his or her capacity as a member of a group:

> "[T]he individual never is considered as an individual, but always in terms of what he has in common with others, such as his motivations, his feelings, or his myths. He is reduced to an average; and, except for a small percentage, action based on averages will be effectual. Moreover, the individual is considered part of the mass and included in it (and so far as possible systematically integrated into it), because in that way his psychic defences are weakened, his reactions are easier to provoke, and the propagandist profits from the process of diffusion of emotions through the mass, and, at the same time, from the pressure felt by an individual when in a group. Emotionalism, impulsiveness, excess, etc. – all these characteristics of the individual caught up in a mass are well known and very helpful to propaganda." (2)

Mass communications, in Eluls's view, strengthen this tendency for the individual to be "alone in the crowd", and the propagandist must use all the media forms currently existing in society:

> "Propaganda tries to surround man by all possible routes, in the realm of feelings as well as ideas, by playing on his will or on his needs, through his conscious and his unconscious, assailing him in both his private and his public life. It furnishes him with a complete system for explaining the world, and provides immediate incentives to action. We are here in the presence of an organized myth that tries to take hold of the entire person. Through the myth it creates, propaganda imposes a complete range of intuitive knowledge, susceptible of only one interpretation, unique and one-sided, and precluding any divergence. This myth becomes so powerful that it invades every area of consciousness, leaving no faculty or motivation intact ... The myth has such motive force that, once accepted, it controls the whole of the individual, who becomes immune to any other influence. This explains the totalitarian attitude that the individual adopts – wherever a myth has been successfully created – and that simply reflects the totalitarian action of propaganda on him ... Propaganda cannot be satisfied with partial successes, for it does not tolerate discussion; by its very nature, it excludes contradiction and discussion." (3)

This propaganda must be unceasing, for only when it completely governs individuals' responses can it make sudden changes which will be believed:

> "Propaganda must be continuous and lasting – continuous in that it must not leave any gaps, but must fill the citizen's whole day and all his days: lasting in that it must function over a very long period of time ... The individual must not be allowed to recover, to collect himself, to remain untouched by propaganda during any relatively long period, for propaganda is not the touch of the magic wand. It is based on slow, constant impregnation. It creates convictions and compliance through imperceptible influences that are effective only by continuous repetition. It must create a total environment for the individual, one from which he never emerges ... The slow building up of reflexes and myths, of psychological environment and prejudices, requires propaganda of very long duration ... Propaganda is a continuous action, without failure or interruption: as soon as the effect of one impulse is weakened, it is renewed by another ... Continuous propaganda exceeds the individual's capacities for attention or adaption and thus his capabilities of resistance. This trait of continuity explains why propaganda can indulge in sudden twists and turns. It is always surprising that the content of propaganda can be so inconsistent that it can approve today what it condemned yesterday ... We must not think that a man ceases to follow the line when there is a sharp turn. He continues to follow it because he is caught up in the system ... Propaganda continues its assault without a instant's respite; his resistance is fragmentary and sporadic. He is caught up in professional tasks and personal preoccupations, and each time he emerges from them he hears and sees the new truth proclaimed. The steadiness of the propaganda prevails over his sporadic attention and makes him follow all the turns from the time he has begun to eat of this bread." (4)

In the contemporary world, Ellul continues, propaganda no longer aims primarily at changing opinions, but to provoke action:

> "The aim of modern propaganda is ... no longer to change adherence to a doctrine, but to make the individual cling irrationally to a process of action. It is no longer to lead to a choice, but to loosen the reflexes. It is no longer to transform an opinion, but to arouse an active and mythical belief ... The propagandist therefore does not normally address himself to the individual's intelligence, for the process of intellectual persuasion is long and uncertain, and the road from such intellectual conviction to action even more so ... Such an action cannot be obtained by the process of choice and deliberation. To be effective, propaganda must constantly short- circuit all thought and decision. It must operate on the individual at the level of the unconscious. He must not know that he is being shaped by outside forces (this is one of the conditions for the success of

propaganda), but some central core in him must be reached in order to release the mechanism in the unconscious which will provide the appropriate – and expected – action ... [T]rue modern propaganda seeks ... to obtain an orthopraxy – an action that in itself, and not because of the value judgments of the person who is acting, leads directly to a goal, which for the individual is not a conscious and intentional objective to be attained, but which is considered such by the propagandist. The propagandist knows what objective should be sought and what action should be accomplished, and he maneuvers the instrument that will secure precisely this action ... Modern psychologists are well aware that there is not necessarily any continuity between conviction and action and no intrinsic rationality in opinions or acts. Into these gaps in continuity propaganda inserts its lever. It does not seek to create wise or reasonable men, but proselytes and militants." (5)

In order for propaganda to be effective, a lengthy process of "pre-propaganda" or "sub-propaganda" is necessary:

"The essential objective of pre-propaganda is to prepare man for a particular action, to make him sensitive to some influence, to get him into condition for the time when he will effectively, and without delay or hesitation, participate in an action ... It proceeds by psychological manipulations, by character modifications, by the creation of feelings or stereotypes useful when the time comes. It must be continuous, slow, imperceptible. Man must be penetrated in order to shape such tendencies. He must be made to live in a certain psychological climate." (6)

And Ellul highlights the following aspect of propaganda:

"Propaganda does not aim to elevate man, but to make him serve. It must therefore utilise the most common feelings, the most widespread ideas, the crudest patterns, and in so doing places itself on a very low level with regard to what it wants man to do and to what end. Hate, hunger and pride make better levers of propaganda than do love or impartiality." (7)

He stresses, however, that propaganda need not necessarily consist of falsehoods. Indeed, the selective use of facts is a far more effective propaganda technique than spreading lies. The propagandist prefers to remain silent about facts that undermine his case rather than lie about them. What is important is that propaganda by-passes the thought process.

Ellul continues:

> "[M]odern man does not think about current problems; he feels them. He reacts, but he does not understand them any more than he takes responsibility for them. He is even less capable of spotting any inconsistency between successive facts; man's capacity to forget is unlimited. This is one of the most important and useful points for the propagandist, who can always be sure that a particular propaganda theme, statement or event will be forgotten within a few weeks." (8)

In recent years, in Britain and elsewhere, a series of alarmist and unjustified health scares has been promoted by a new class of professional health activists which has both a vested interest in the continuing discovery of new scares and an agenda hostile to individual liberty and the free market and favourable to greater state control and restrictions on freedom.

The existence of such health scares is unsurprising in a society dominated, as Professor Ellul demonstrated, by propaganda. What is of most concern is the fact that professional scientists have been brought in to "validate" some of the most spurious claims involved in these scares. The danger to the integrity and prestige of the scientific profession should not be underestimated.

We will now examine a selection of these health scares. We hope that both scientists and members of the public will look with greater skepticism on the dissemination of wild claims which have either not been subjected to, or not withstood, the rigours of testing under scientific conditions. We hope too, that the political and ideological purposes behind the manufacture of pseudo-scientific scares will also become clear, and that the media might become less a conduit for propaganda and more a source of unsullied and objective information.

III: ON FOOD FASCISM

As with the anti-smoking movement, "food fascism" is not just a recent phenomenon. It can certainly be traced back to the pre-War era.

For example, in the 1930s, Sir John Boyd Orr, director of the Rowett Nutritional Institute, in his study *Family, Health and Income*, argued that a high fat diet, that is, one composed primarily of meat, milk and dairy products, was a healthy diet, on the evidence of studies which showed that upper-class children at Christus Hospital public school were on average taller than working-class children attending state schools. The Christus Hospital children had a higher fat diet than did the working-class children, and Boyd Orr claimed, probably correctly, that this led to them growing taller. However, Boyd Orr and many politicians went far beyond this to claim that large sections of the working class were undernourished and thus in poor health. In 1936, during a Commons debate on "the growing evidence of widespread malnutrition ... and the continued failure of His Majesty's Government to take effective steps to deal with the unjust problem of hunger and want in the midst of plenty", Boyd Orr's studies were cited as showing that "there were nine million people in the country whose diet was defective in 'protective' constituents". (9)

Yet there was no evidence to support this contention. Indeed, in 1938, a detailed physical examination of many children across the social classes revealed no marked discrepancies in health. Although working class children were generally of shorter stature, there was no difference in the incidence of anaemia, rickets, vitamin deficiencies and so on. Despite this, official policy sought to encourage the populace to eat a high-fat diet on the grounds that it would improve health, in place of supposedly "poor quality" foods such as bread and potatoes.

The real 'take-off' of food fascism, however, occurred in the mid-1960s, when an apparently new illness, coronary heart disease, was killing thousands of men prematurely. This disease was almost unknown in the mid-1920s, but had increased exponentially in incidence every year to become the commonest form of premature death in males. The hypothesis was proposed that a high fat diet, resulting in cholesterol infiltrating the walls of the arteries to the heart, was the cause of this disease. In consequence, a low fat diet was officially promoted as the "new healthy diet". Statistical evidence was presented in order to support this claim, but, as Dr. James Le Fanu, a London general practitioner and medical columnist, puts it:

"Put bluntly, the facts have been selected and edited, preventing their proper interpretation and it is not surprising that when we turn to the circumstantial evidence that is held to underpin the relationship between a high fat diet and heart disease we find it has been similarly edited". (10)

For example, the health activists point to the fact that the rate of heart disease increases in Japanese immigrants to the United States as they increase the amount of fat in their diet. The claim is made that this is due to the fact that they have exchanged the traditional low-fat diet of Japan for the high-fat diet common in the US. Yet the Swedes have similar levels of fat consumption compared to the US, but lower heart disease rates. When Swedes emigrated to the US, their heart disease rates doubled even though the amount of fat in their diet remained the same. In fact, there is a generalised phenomenon that migrants lose the patterns of disease of their native country and acquire those of their adoptive country. Thus the rates of common Japanese diseases like stomach cancer and stroke fall as Japanese migrate to the US, while low incidence diseases like heart disease and breast cancer rise to the levels of their adoptive country. It is, in short, a misrepresentation to claim the evidence shows that increased fat consumption causes heart disease, just as in the 1930s it was a misrepresentation to claim that the evidence showed that increased fat consumption led to better health.

Dr. Le Fanu thus concludes that:

"Nutritional wisdoms about healthy diet are utopian, their attraction is that they fulfil the need of individuals and societies to improve themselves. The utopian response to the depression of the 1930s was to demand that all should embrace the nutritional habits of the upper class with a diet high in dairy foods. The utopian response to the affluence of the 1960s is based on the supposition that prosperity is harmful and that harm can be mitigated by an ascetic diet that spurns high fat foods in favour of cereals, fibres, bread and pasta." (11)

1: Food Fascism as Surrogate Socialism

In part, the activities of the health activists represent a shift from the traditional, discredited, form of socialism, which involved the nationalisation of private industry and business. Instead they are constructing a new form of political control through, first, much greater state regulation and higher taxation, and, second, by opening up vast new scope for lawsuits through increasing company liability under the guise of "consumer protection". Anwar Fazal, former president of the International Organisation of Consumer Unions, said that "Nothing short of a revolution will substantially alter the character of the business system and its ally advertising." He added that "that revolution has now begun the world over", and went on:

> "With our new way of global organising, and with our new power, multinationals will have to change on a significant level.
>
> We have now got muscle globally to deal with them in a way that we never had before: power to organise globally, to organise boycotts, direct actions, shareholder actions, power to embarrass them for engaging in unconscionable activities." (12)

The health activists have not repudiated central planning; they have simply transferred it from the economy, where it has repeatedly been proved catastrophic, to society, the lifestyle and everyday habits of the people. Old style socialists and power-mongers wanted to nationalise industries. Their modern counterparts are seeking to nationalise civil society. To replace the realm of private space and private life by "co-ordinated plans", "encouragement", "education" (i.e., propaganda), "guidelines" to ensure that people adopt "healthy" lifestyles and diets.

2: The Institutionalisation and Assumptions of Food Fascism

The institutionalisation of food fascism in Britain, and health fascism in general, has occurred with the almost universal political and intellectual acceptance of the "Health of the Nation" programme. In the 1991 a British government Green Paper, entitled The Health of the Nation, targets were set for a 30% reduction in coronary heart disease by the year 2000. The proposed means for achieving this was by reducing the proportion of the population eating high levels of fats from 85% to 50%.

Four breathtaking assumptions undergird the *Health of the Nation* approach:

- The first is that the individual eating decisions of millions of different people is something legitimately subject to central planning by Whitehall.

- The second is that one particular alteration to diet will reduce the risk of coronary heart disease of every single one of these millions of individuals, regardless of their differences in age, sex, physiology, metabolism, medical history, occupation, genetic inheritance, psychological and emotional make-up, lifestyle, income, family situation and dozens of other factors.

- The third is that a high-fat diet does in fact increase an individual's risk of developing coronary heart disease, a claim which is not supported by the existing evidence, as we shall see below.

- The fourth is that either the appropriate proportion of these millions of people will obediently change their diets on schedule in order to please the authors of the government paper, or, presumably, that bureaucrats will use coercive measures to compel individuals to eat the food the bureaucrats want them to.

Traditional British liberal ideas that every individual should enjoy freedom of choice, control over his or her life, and the right to inform himself or herself of the facts about health and diet and take action accordingly, is directly contradicted by the thinking behind such documents as *The Health of the Nation.*

Nor is it the case that state regulation of the food the people eat is carried out in accordance with objective scientific criteria, entirely separate from the vested interests of state bureaucrats, politicians, health activists, food producers and food retailers. The proponents of food fascism portray themselves as Simon-pure embodiments of the "public interest". Their view of the state is problematical. On the one hand they constantly portray it as being led astray and corrupted by the vested interests of capitalist industry and agriculture. On the other hand, as their own influence within it grows, every allegedly "objective" report (i.e., one favouring their viewpoint) or "health promoting" policy is welcomed, and further state supremacy coercion of the individual welcomed.

The reality of all government policy making is, as the "public choice", economics of politics, analysis shows, rather more complicated. As Catherine Montgomery Blight, a solicitor and economist, and Simon Scanlan, an agricultural economist, both of the School of Agriculture, Edinburgh, argue, "a market for regulation" exists "superimposed on the market for actual products."

As they further point out:

> "It is not just a simple matter of answering the demand 'There ought to be a law ...'. Certainly, the supply of the regulation is derived from the legislature and its delegated agencies. It is they who have the power to enact laws, rules and regulations. The source of the demand for regulation is any interest which sees a possible advantage in obtaining a particular regulation. In other words, the market for regulation is best understood as part of the competitive process. Regulation therefore occurs because there are well-organised interests which expect to benefit. Trade organisations lobby in Parliament, in the press, through public relations activities. Sometimes, unexpected coalitions arise between, for example, industry

and consumer groups, overtly opposed, but covertly acting in concert. From time to time, we see members of interest groups forming associations and disbanding to align with others, as circumstances and motives change. Within this framework, officials and bureaucrats play a subtle role, which is rarely obvious. It manifests itself in the bias which such officials show towards regulatory solutions to problems. A more obvious part is played by the dominant firms in an industry. Several writers argue that specific regulations can be proved to give a competitive advantage to the dominant firm, by raising its rivals' costs. Thus, the much vaunted benefits which accrue to consumers from the recent legislation on food labelling should be taken with more than a pinch of salt. What has happened is that food processing companies have actually accepted rules on labelling which suit them." (13)

3: Food Scares – 57 Varieties?

Let us now survey what is merely a selection of the claims with which the public is bombarded every day, from reports in daily newspapers:

"Vested Interests 'Push Deadly Diet'"

"Farmers, the food industry, and government were all blamed yesterday for inflicting a deadly fatty diet on the British. "Major institutional forces" are inhibiting a shift to healthier diet which could radically cut early death from cancer and heart disease, Professor Philip James, an authority on the links between diet and disease, told a conference in London ... People had been made aware of salmonella and other food hygiene problems, but the much bigger danger of a poor diet high in fat and sugar was being concealed from them. Dr. James, who sits on most government health panels and directs the Rowett Research Institute for nutrition, said food labels were unfathomable to the average consumer." (*The Guardian*, 12th December 1990)

"Toast Joins Cancer Danger-List Foods".

"Mushrooms, pepper, celery, coffee, potatoes and even toast contain substances that can cause cancer, according to a study in the latest issue of the magazine Science ...'There are a large number of mutagens (gene-damaging substances) and carcinogens in every meal ..." (*The Scotsman*, 17 September 1986)

"Study Reveals Danger from a Pinch of Salt"

"A new study reporting higher health risks posed by salt shows that reduced consumption could prevent around 70,000 deaths a year in Britain. A daily individual reduction of three grammes – by avoiding salty foods and not adding salt to food in cooking or at the table – would be more effective than drugs in lowering blood pressure. But the study's conclusions, published in the *British Medical Journal*, stress that food manufacturers must also reduce the levels and list the amount of salt in processed food." (*The Guardian*, 5th September 1991)

"Barbecued Meat Can be Linked to Cancer"

"Meat fried or barbecued for long periods and at high temperatures produces substances that have induced cancer in several species of animals, including monkeys, a scientist from the American National Cancer Institute has reported." (*The Times*, 27th March 1991)

Celia Hall, "Pickled Food Linked With Throat Cancer".

"Eating too many pickled onions increases the risk of throat cancer and a preference for taking very hot soup or drinks as well will increase the risk further." (*The Independent*, 29 May 1992)

"Waldegrave Backs Advice to Cut Sugar"

"There is virtually no need to eat any fats and sugar, and people eat much more protein and salt than is good for them, according to a report by the Government's panel on nutrition published yesterday. The report urges sweeping changes in Britain's unhealthy diet and confirms the links between bad eating habits and disease. Its recommendations, endorsed yesterday by the Health Secretary, William Waldegrave, echo advice from the World Health Organisation in April and exceed guidelines in The Health of the Nation, the Government's consultation paper published last month ... The report ... is the first comprehensive government guide to the amounts of nutrients people should eat." (*The Guardian*, 10th July 1991)

"Chocs as Wicked as Cigs." (*The Daily Mirror*, 30 March, 1994, p. 5)

"Chocoholics' Cravings Confirmed as Chronic". (*The Daily Telegraph*, 21 March, 1994)

"Sweet Danger".

"(I)t has been recognised since 1970 that licorice taken in quantities can cause high blood pressure ... sudden cardiac arrest, congested cardiac failure and, more prosaically, headaches [are] possible complications of heavy licorice consumption" (*The Times*, 25 May 1995, p. 17)

"Alert Over Slim Drinks."

"More than half of Britain's teenage girls are at risk from bone disease because they prefer fizzy slimming drinks to milkshakes." (*Today*, 28 March 1992)

"TV is Blamed For the Junk-Food Generation"

"Television was blamed yesterday for spawning a junk-food generation of children deliberately coaxed away from healthy eating. Slick advertising and promotional gimmicks for fast foods and sweets have helped hold down the standard of children's diets for the past decade, says a new survey ... Education chiefs are now launching a counter-attack to challenge the dominance of the multinationals." (*The Evening Standard*, 27th July 1992)

"Coffee and Tea 'Are As Bad as Fags'".

"Tea, coffee, sugar and alcohol are 'social poisons' as bad as cigarette, a health group [Women's Nutritional Advisory Service] claimed yesterday". (*The Sun*, 25 March, 1993)

Charles Laurence, "US Spreading the Bad News on Margarine."

"Margarine can be as bad for the heart as butter, according to an American government study". (*The Daily Telegraph*, 8 October 1992, p. 8)

"Researchers Warn of Heart Risk in Hard Margarine"

"A group of Dutch researchers claim that hard margarine is as likely to cause heart disease as butter or lard." (*The Guardian*, 17th August 1990)

"Cancer Link to Chinese Food".

"Scientists in Hong King have linked certain Chinese foods to lung cancer". (*The Sunday Times,* 18 June 1995)

"Sugar Trade School Pack Criticised"

"Educational packs produced by the sugar industry for teachers to use in the classroom have been attacked by a group of doctors, dentists and nutritionists which condemns them as a marketing gimmick. The Action and Information on Sugars group claims that the 75-page pack, produced by Tate & Lyle and the British Sugar Corporation, encourages children to consume sugar against the latest Government advice that intake should be drastically cut ... Professor Aubrey Sheiham, of University College, London, and a member of AIS, said: ... 'For a commercially-orientated group to issue material which is encouraging activities detrimental to health is of grave concern." (*The Daily Telegraph*, 9th September 1991)

"TV Soaps Dish Up the Bad Food Guide"

"Characters in Australian soap operas are setting British television audiences a bad example by eating and drinking themselves sick, a nutritionist says in *The Food Magazine*, published today by the Food Commission. Heather Morton, head of nutrition and social health at the University of South Australia, analysed 45 hours of three Australian television series popular with young British audiences, Neighbours, Home and Away and A Country Practice. Though their characters are seen as epitomes of clean, modern, fresh-faced living, Dr. Morton says, they spend a quarter of their time eating and drinking. They also purvey misinformation about food and drink, and insidiously promote brands such as Coca-Cola and Foster's lager ... [W]hen the characters talked about food and drink more than half their statements were rubbish, Dr. Morton found. All the food-related remarks she analysed concerned body-image and slimming. All were made by women and on 43 per cent were scientifically correct. Dr. Morton also criticises attitudes to alcohol. Though the programmes never showed young people drinking alcohol, 'generally alcohol drinking was presented as normal and non-problematic'." (*The Times*, 15th January 1991)

"Meat Eaters Blamed for Damaging Planet"

"Richer lifestyles and increased consumption are responsible for between half and three-quarters of environmental damage in the West caused by natural habitat and air pollution. Meat eaters are particularly to blame ... A conference in London organised by the third world charity ActionAid on 'lifestyle overload' was told that Westerners needed to adopt leaner and less materialistic lifestyles to combat environmental problems caused by population growth. These include smaller cars, better public transport and a tax system which brings more benefit to the poor." (*The Independent*, 21st November 1991)

"Pollution: Smoking Burgers Up the Air".

"They're small, smelly and smoggy. Cigarettes and hamburgers have been blamed for a lot of ills, but now they're being accused of helping cause an entirely different health problem: the Los Angeles' smog ...

Cigarette and barbecued hamburger smoke gives off much the same sized particles of smut as cars or fires. But [Glen] Cass and his group [at the California Institute of Technology in Pasadena] were amazed to find just how bad the problem is: cigarette smoke makes up about one per cent and hamburger smoke about four per cent of the fine particles polluting the Los Angeles air ...

The message is clear: turn vegetarian and give up smoking if you want a good view of the horizon". (*The Guardian*, 15 September 1994, p. 3)

"Peril in a Bread Roll: Can Hot Dogs Cause Leukemia?"

"Research has linked high consumption of hot dogs with an increase in childhood leukemia." (*The Times*, 23 June 1994, p. 17)

And one's sense of *schadenfreude* is satisfied by the fact that even the pursuit of health and fitness does not appear to be riskless, as the following press coverage reveals:

"MPs Warn Against Diets".

38 MPs signed a Commons motion about "the perils and futility of dieting, except for medical reasons", criticised the "tyranny of thinness", "sexist judgment of women on the basis of looks" and the "oppression of fat people" in support of International No Diet Day. (*The Times*, 6 May 1993)

"They're Eating Not Much, Much Too Young"

Diet Breakers charity has been established to warn young people of the dangers of excessive and obsessive dieting. It was vital to "target children aged nine or 10 at the latest", according to principal clinical psychologist, Dr., Bryant-Waugh, a coordinator of "the eating disorder research team", at Great Ormond Street Children's Hospital. (*The Independent*, 15 August 1994, p. 18)

"The Health Drink Trap: Parents Who Feed Children Fruit Juice and Squash Can Stunt Their Growth, Say Experts". (*The Daily Mail*, 15 February, 1995 p. 3)

"Dieting 'Could Cause Violent Behaviour.'"

"A diet that cuts the production of the brain chemical serotonin may boost aggressive behaviour, according to a study announced yesterday at an international meeting ... " (*The Daily Telegraph*, 13 November 1995)

"Low Fat Diet Linked to Male Suicide."

"Men with low cholesterol levels are more likely to take their own lives than those with higher fat levels, according to a study in the *British Medical Journal* today". (*The Guardian*, 31 July 1992)

"Herb Teas Linked With Liver Deaths". (*The Times*, 11 September, 1992)

"Joggers More Likely to Have Fatigue Says Doctor".

"Joggers are at increased risk of developing post-disease viral fatigue syndrome, the mystery disease thought particularly to affect 'high-fliers', a doctor has discovered." (*The Daily Telegraph*, 19th December 1988)

"Men in Peril of Being Too Fit."

"Men who over-exercise have lower hormone levels and may be doing their bodies and minds more harm than good, Canadian researchers who carried out a study on exercise reported last week". (*The Times*, 14 December 1991)

"Greens May Not Be So Good for You After All."

"Professor Clive West and Mr. Sdakia de Pee [of the Wageningen Agricultural University] have led a team in an investigation that defies the popular belief [that greens are good for you], and concludes that a diet with lots of green, leafy vegetables does not boost vitamin A levels". (*Western Daily Press*, 13 July 1995, p. 7)

"Veggie Burger Killed Student".

"Kerry Foster, 18, a first-year student at Kent University, died from an allergic reaction to walnuts after eating a veggie burger in her college canteen ... the nuts had caused Kerry's mouth to swell, cutting off her air supply." (*The Daily Telegraph*, 12 December 1992)

4: The Realities of Health and Diet

Needless to say, the casual newspaper reader or television viewer would in all likelihood gain the impression that the average British diet is a minefield of deadly poisons.

But the reality is that there can be no doubt that the population of the Western world today enjoys longer life-spans, better health and lower rates of infant mortality than any population at any time in history. The health prospects and life expectancy of the average baby born in the West today are a dramatic improvement over what they were in any previous century (or even the early years of this century). It is a reasonable assumption that the diet eaten by the people who enjoy this remarkable health success story must be conducive to good health (or, at worst, neutral in its health effects). As Professor Marks puts it:

"It is almost invariably forgotten (or more likely, deliberately suppressed) by those who attribute a purported but unsubstantiated deterioration in food quality to scientific and industrial intervention, that it was just such intervention that produced the revolution in food production, preparation and preservation earlier in this century, from which we are still continuing to benefit and which enables the world to support a population many times larger than was ever possible before. Without access to modern agricultural methods and the industrial packaging, processing and handling of food – which we now accept as commonplace – the likelihood of the countries in the EEC being self-sufficient in food for its 250 million or so inhabitants, would be extremely low, and the ability to feed the populace of large cities such as London and Paris, would be non-existent." (14)

Professor Donald J. McNamara, of the department of nutrition and food science at the University of Arizona in Tucson, remarks of the claims of health propaganda in relation to food that "Overall nutritional quality, balance and moderation, and the four food groups have been replaced by an attitude that certain foods cause disease while other foods prevent disease, and that what one eats, rather than supplying nutrients and being one of life's pleasures, is a major determinant of the cause of one's mortality." (15)

Yet the health activists, through the manufacture of health scares, are making ever greater demands for state restrictions on the production, distribution, sale and consumption of foodstuffs. The public is engulfed with a deluge of propaganda, largely at the taxpayers' expense, about supposedly "good" and "bad" foods. Dr. Digby Anderson, Director of the Social Affairs Unit, writes:

"The evidence relating diet to health is not conclusive. Indeed much of what is presented to the public even in supposedly official reports such as that of the National Advisory Council on Nutritional Education (NACNE) or by quasi-official bodies such as the Health Education Council, is not strictly scientific. There is no single clear, simple message about fat, salt, sugar and fibre or even about body weight agreed and packaged by scientists and ready for popular dissemination. There is no guarantee that if we change our diet to avoid allegedly unhealthy food that all, even many of us will enjoy better health let alone live longer. Indeed some such changes might even make some people less healthy. Interference by the Government in the agricultural market has so far led to the production of more not less 'unhealthy' foods and it is better to leave the choice of what to eat to individuals. Banning advertisements for foods decreed 'unhealthy' would not help wiser eating.

"In short, the public is being deceived by those who push a simplistic health message identifying good and bad foods for all in the name of science and arguing for Government food controls. The state of scientific knowledge does provide much on which thoughtful consumers might ponder. There is a case for a balanced diet. Some individuals need specialised advice. There is a need for health education. But there is no justification, scientific or otherwise for crude propaganda about supposedly bad and good foods fired aimlessly at the total population at public expense." (16)

5: The Cholesterol Cacophony

In America the anti-cholesterol message has even been enacted in outright public bans. Thus, Sausalito City Council, California, has established a 22 "cholesterol free zones", where restaurants are required by law to offer "no-cholesterol" food to patrons. And the State of New Jersey banned restaurants from serving runny or raw eggs or dishes that use uncooked eggs, such as Caesar salads or mayonnaise. (17) In Britain the Health Education Authority (HEA) and Coronary Prevention Group campaign for mass cholesterol testing.

What is especially notable, however, is how the health propandists rush to rubbish any evidence that contradicts their views or complicates it. A study of 15000 people in Scotland in the *British Medical Journal* in April 1985, which showed that those with low levels of cholesterol in their blood was offset by a higher risk of cancer! "We conclude that it may be a mistake to assume that dietary advice given to the general population to reduce the intake of saturated fat will necessarily reduce overall mortality. Coronary heart disease may well de crease but other risks might increase." (18)

The fact is that it is impossible to simply classify a substance as "safe" or "toxic", implying that this is true regardless of dose and the individual's own situation. For instance, in 1990 the *British Medical Journal* reported the case of a man who nearly died after eating a vegieburger containing, unbeknown to him, peanuts, to which he knew he was allergic and normally avoided. Most people consider substances such as arsenic, cyanide and strychnine as poisons; yet on a weight-for-weight basis they are far less damaging than many essential components of the diet, such as vitamin D and selenium. Paracelsus, the 16th-century German chemist and father of toxicology, said that to talk of toxicity without reference to dose is meaningless. The human body requires certain trace dietary substances, collectively known as vitamins and essential minerals (or trace elements). Illnesses can occur if an individual's diet is deficient in one or more of these substances. Therefore, in the words of Professor Marks:

> "Since the 30 or so trace substances of dietary origin that are now known to be essential for a full and healthy life are not evenly distributed in different foodstuffs, the only way to ensure that they are all taken in adequate amounts is to eat as varied a diet as possible ... It was already known before the Second World War that anyone eating a variety of foodstuffs in amounts sufficient to maintain their bodyweight within reasonable limits was unlikely to have a nutritionally related disease. If they did, it was good evidence of an underlying illness such as malabsorption requiring medical rather than dietary treatment. This knowledge about what constitutes a healthy diet has still not been improved upon." (19)

We have seen above how from the 1930s the propaganda of the health activists argued – without real scientific proof – that the state should encourage people to consume a high-fat diet. From the 1960s the greatly increased volume of propaganda began arguing – again without scientific proof – that such a diet was harmful to health and that the state should do all in its power to encourage people to consume a low-fat diet. According to Dr. Barbara Pickard, honorary research fellow in the department of animal physiology and nutrition at Leeds University:

> "The end result of all this is a belief system which is almost totally unrelated to scientific fact; it is the child who when offered a drink of milk refused on the grounds that it might give him a heart attack; it is the housewife who believes margarine is less fattening than butter and who dare not eat red meat although it might cure her anaemia; it is the middle-aged man who denies himself any visible animal fat, supremely confident that this will insure him against heart disease, and happily oblivious of the insidious undermining of his health caused by his aggres-

sions, frustrations and inability to sleep properly. Even more dangerous, it is those individuals in positions of power, in medicine, politics and the food industry who seem to be forming their opinions from the popular press and television rather than from reasoned scientific publications." (20)

In 1974 the Department of Health and Social Security (DHSS) committee on medical aspect of food policy concluded that no single dietary factor could be regarded as predominant in determining susceptibility to heart disease. And in 1978, the DHSS book Eating for Health recommended a diet which should comprise "a mixture of many different foods and include cereal foods, protein foods, some fat (to ensure essential fatty acids) and fruit and vegetables" (21)

However, in 1985, the Joint Advisory Committee on Nutrition Education (JACNE) stated that "The main problem as far as your heart is concerned is too much saturated fat" (22). Dr. Pickard asks:

"In the decade between the sensible and cautious Eating for Health and the JACNE leaflet, had a welter of new research evidence appeared? It would seem not and, if anything, later evidence has merely added further to the confusion ... Consensus is the slogan of the health education movement; consistency of message has come to assume greater importance than the fundamental issue of whether the message is correct." (23)

Indeed, when a comparison between the consumption of animal fats and deaths from coronary heart disease in different countries is made, no incriminating pattern appears. Studies within countries are similarly inconclusive in causal terms, and trends in animal fat consumption over time are not causally related. The blanket dietary advice is aimed at virtually everybody except children under five; however, they may not be of benefit to some, and could be harmful to others, including growing children, active adults and women who are pregnant, breastfeeding or contemplating pregnancy. Indeed, a report on diet and cancer from the National Academy of Sciences (in the United States) argues that whole milk protects against some forms of cancer. Dr. Pickard cites the example of a 50-year-old American businessman who enjoyed excellent health until he started to virtually abstain from milk and cheese through fear of heart disease. He then started to suffer from hypertension, which several months of drug therapy failed to cure. A doctor then advised him to liberalise his diet to include more dairy produce and achieve an intake of one gram of calcium daily. Within two weeks of this new diet, his blood pressure was normal, drugs were discontinued, and six weeks later all side-effects had disappeared. Dr. McCarron, reporting on this case, commented:

> "It is thus important for physicians to realise, in our present state of ignorance about the causation of the major chronic disorders, that variety and moderation in diet is the best advice for all reasonably healthy persons. Imbalances can be caused by over-zealous practices of dietary restriction which adversely affect the overall health of the individual." (24)

The hypothesis that diet causes heart disease has been thoroughly tested in the largest and most expensive set of trials in the history of medicine. In Europe and the United States, 60,000 middle-aged men were recruited for massive control trials in which half were encouraged to reduce their fat consumption, stop smoking and be treated for high blood pressure if necessary (the 'intervention' group), while the remaining 30,000 acted as controls. There were four such trials: MRFIT and WHO in men with normal cholesterol levels, and the OSLO and LRCCPPT in men with abnormally high levels of cholesterol in the blood. In the MRFIT and WHO trials, the recommendations to reduce fat consumption had no effect on either mortality from heart disease or total mortality. In the OSLO and LRCCPT trial the risk of heart disease was reduced in the intervention group, but only down to the level of the rest of the population, and there was no difference in total mortality. Similarly, in the province of Karelia, in Finland, the authorities encouraged people to adopt a low fat diet in order to reduce the level of heart disease. Although heart disease did fall during the period of the study, it was also falling throughout Finland (for unknown reasons), and at the end of the project Karelia still had the country's highest rate of heart disease and the decline was no greater than in a "control" province, Kuopio. Since 1968 there has been a dramatic decline in heart disease in several countries, particularly Australia, New Zealand, Canada, the US and Japan; yet in none of these countries has the decline been accompanied by a radical change in fat consumption.

In 1993, the French National Institute for Health and Medical Research (Inserm) published the results of a four-year study of 600 cardiac patients in Lyons. Half of the volunteers in the study followed the conventional recommended diet for heart attack victims – virtually vegetarian, high in polyunsaturated fats like margarine and sunflower oil, and alcohol-free – while the other 300 followed a far more varied "Mediterranean" diet which included olive or rapeseed oil instead of polyunsaturates and allowed meat once a day, fish twice a week and a glass or two of wine with meals. The study was supposed to last five years, but was terminated after four years on ethical grounds: the rate of deaths from second heart attacks among those following the medically recommended diet was five to six times higher than among those on the varied "Mediterranean" diet. (25)

Indeed, while the French eat as much animal fat, have as much cholesterol in their blood, and smoke about as much as the British, drink vastly more wine and take little exercise, the rate of premature heart disease among French men is lower than in any industrialised country except Japan. French women do even better, with one of the world's lowest rates of death from heart disease. And the French heart attack rate is actually falling further. In the United States, there was a remarkable increase in heart disease up to a peak in 1963, and, since then, an equally remarkable decline; yet cholesterol levels have remained virtually unchanged, despite the fact that Americans have drastically reduced their intake of animal fat.

Professor Serge Renaud, one of France's leading epidemiologists, has carried out detailed studies of 2,500 middle-aged men who do not yet suffer from heart disease in Northern Ireland, where Ulstermen die prematurely of heart attacks at a rate of 348 per 100,000 of the population, and of 2,500 of their counterparts in the city of Toulouse, where men die of this complaint at a rate of only 78 per 100,000. These studies found that the French have high levels of vitamin C in their blood, while some Ulstermen have levels of vitamin C so low as to put them at risk of scurvy, according to Professor Alun Evans, a leading British epidemiologist. Professor Renaud believes that vitamins from vegetable and fruit may be just as relevant in determining who suffers from heart disease as either high cholesterol or smoking, and recommends that a healthy diet to ward off heart disease should consist of traditional foods, carefully cooked, slowly eaten and washed down with red wine. "In Toulouse they consume more bread, more vegetables and fruit, less butter, more cheese, more vegetable fat and more wine," he says. "They eat what our grandparents ate – and, like our grandparents, not many of them die young of coronary heart disease." (26)

And Professor McNamara notes that:

> "The outcome of much of the scientific debate with its public exposure and the pronouncements from pseudo-nutritionists is a confused and cynical public. What should an individual do to reduce his or her risk of heart disease? First find out which risk factors exist and which ones can be reduced by some sort of intervention ... These are basic questions which require more of the patient than to give up eating eggs, red meats, and dairy products; however, they also have the potential of making significant changes in that patient's heart disease risk profile. And of even greater potential benefit is that this approach treats those who need treatment in an effective, patient-specific manner and allows the rest of us to feel less guilty and apprehensive about what we are having for dinner tonight." (27)

One problem is that the assumption that the cause of coronary heart disease has already been identified may divert attention and funds away from research projects in this area. Dr. Pickard continues:

> "Another area of concern has to do with the growing spectre of legislation and regulations on diet. If the diet evangelists have their way, such bureaucratic threats may become reality, regardless of the weakness of the scientific evidence. Furthermore, those critical of restrictions of individual freedom in other countries would do well to focus attention on the insidious development in this country of propaganda-type broadcasting on dietary issues. It is astonishing that the deliberations of TV and radio producers and presenters are more influential than those of full-time professionals working on diet and disease ... Puzzled milk producers, still staggering from the imposition of quota restrictions by the EEC, now face even further economic hardships as a result of falling

consumption ... After investing heavily to produce more and more, the farmer may now be saddled with a lifetime burden of debt, a debt which government actively encouraged him to take on. Industries which depend on the livestock industry, such as machinery manufacturers and suppliers of animal feeds, all face cutbacks too." (28)

The war over cholesterol continues, however. In February of 1995 Professor Nicholas Wald, Professor of Epidemiology at St. Bartholomews Hospital, announced results of a meta-analysis that, in his words, "confirmed" (a word that astute readers of health propaganda should recognise as a red light that something contentious and disputable is being asserted), that high blood cholesterol is associated with increased risk of heart attack. He also claimed that reducing it by as little as 10% could reduce the risk of coronary by a quarter. In reality, meta- analysis is a rather dodgy epidemiological technique, and open to gross methodological errors and opportunities for deliberate slanting and massage of results (as the case of the "passive smoking" scam has so clearly demonstrated) (29). At the same time as Professor Wald's confident pronouncement the research of Dr. Fred Kern at the University of Colorado Medical School has been pointing to the role of our biological homeostatic mechanism, the way in which our metabolisms maintain physiological states at a steady state, and hence resisting attempts to influence those states by dietary alterations. (30)

Professor Wald's confident assertions have to be seen against the reality of the background of the growing critique of the cholesterol orthodoxy and its media amen corner. An honourable exception to the general reliance on establishment press release medicine has been the Science Correspondent of The Times, Nigel Hawkes, whose columns have, over a period of time, ably presented the anomalies that confront the cholesterol paradigm, and the growing researches that challenge it.

Thus, speaking of the "hole in the heart of the cholesterol cult", Hawkes has denounced such propaganda splurges as the Family Heart Association's "Cholesterol Countdown Week" as "mischievous, misleading and wrong". (31)

He thus declared that:

> "To judge by the confident manner of the campaigners for healthy eating, one might assume that their recipes had been proved in large-scale trials. But, as Professor Michael Oliver of the Royal Brompton Hospital has pointed out, there has never been a controlled trial of low-fat diets in healthy people,

> Different considerations apply to those who have already survived heart attacks, or to people with extra-high levels of cholesterol in their blood-stream cause by their genes. But for the average Joe, low-fat diets are both extremely inefficient at reducing cholesterol level and of unproven efficacy in cutting the death rate. For Joe's wife, less prone to heart disease, the argument is feebler. The point never seems to register.

> For a start, the relationship between fats in the diet and the prevalence of heart disease is very rough and ready. Britons may indeed eat too much fat, but heart disease statistics fail to prove it. The areas with the highest heart deaths – Scotland and the North – do not have a fattier diet than the rest of us. The rich eat more fat, and have higher cholesterol levels, but suffer less heart disease than the poor.

> There is a link between high cholesterol levels and the risk of heart disease, but there is an equally strong association with another factor found in the blood, fibrinogen. But because high fibrinogen levels cannot be blamed on individual greed or a refusal to accept advice, they have been almost entirely ignored. Cholesterol, and its link with fat, has achieved an eminence largely unjustified by the scientific data.

> What the dietary advice really amounts to is a national experiment with results that cannot be predicted. People who have taken it seriously and plunged into polyunsaturates could be doing more harm than good. There is growing evidence that over-emphasis on the plant-based acids, the omega-6 series used to make margarines, can upset the balance of the diet". (32)

Hawkes has similarly denounced the *Health of the Nation* dietary guidelines as "laughable to anybody not in thrall to the nutritional nostrums that first gained a foothold 20 years ago", and pointed out how they ignore the increasingly apparent benefits of anti-oxidants and wine (33). And he has publicised the researches of critical scientists like Michael Oliver of Royal Brampton National Heart and

Lung Institute, who has declared:

> "Government, health department and many health educationists are rigid in the belief that reducing dietary fat is beneficial ... vast sums of money are being spent on nutritional programmes, dieting advice and nurse counselling which may be completely ineffectual".

Hawkes also cited 6 recent trials where no benefits in reduced deaths from heart disease or other any causes came from reducing saturated fats. In his view the "lipid hypothesis" of heart disease, of high fat leading to high levels of cholesterol in the bloodstream with consequently increased risks of arterial blockages, can be challenged by the "Oxidised LDL hypothesis". The latter would suggest that it is not cholesterol per se that does harm, but that part linked to low-density lipoproteins (LDL) which becomes oxidised in the body. A therapeutic alternative to be drawn from this hypothesis would emphasise the role of anti-oxidant vitamins. (34)

Another distinguished critic of the cholesterol establishment is the General Practitioner and medical columnist and author Dr. James Le Fanu. In a number of articles, and in his book *Eat Your Heart Out: The Fallacy of the Healthy Diet* (35) Le Fanu has exposed the "partisanship with which the diet-disease thesis has been promoted in the medical journals" and the consequent "process of selection and suppression of the relevant evidence". As he has declared:

> "[T]he protagonists were defence, prosecution, judge and jury of their own theories ... there was no independent judge of the diet-disease thesis because those promoting it were in the position to ensure that the evidence disproving it was kept out of the realms of public knowledge." (36)

Fortunately, however, as in all such cases of suppression and propaganda, it has proved impossible to prevent the gradual emergence of competing evidence in medical literature or the general media. Thus in the *British Medical Journal*, U. Ravnskov has shown how "Authors of papers on preventing coronary heart disease by lowering blood cholesterol values tend to cite only trials with positive results. The impression of success presented to doctors is false because the numbers of controlled cholesterol lowering trials in which total mortality was reduced equals the numbers in which there were increases." (37)

And even the arguments of Professors Paul Abernathy and David Black of Purdue University in that obesity is not necessarily unhealthy (in an article in The Journal of the American Dietetic Association) have been reported: "Heightweight tables may have little meaning for individuals and may cause more harm than good". Fat does not simply gather round the body as an energy store, they argue. It also removes harmful substances, such as fatty acids and cholesterol. (38)

6: The Salt Scare

Food alarmism has hardly been confined to the issue of cholesterol, however.

In the 1950s and early 60s, Louis Dahl advanced the hypothesis that consumption of salt was a cause of hypertension (high blood pressure), claiming that there was a direct relationship between the incidence of hypertension and the use of salt throughout the world. He bred a strain of rat which became hypertensive when a large amount of sodium was given with its food. Dahl's hypothesis was not widely accepted at the time, as the anthropological data on which it was based was too uncertain, and the Dahl strain of rat had little in common with other forms of hypertension in laboratory animals. Only in the late 1970s did enthusiasm emerge for the Dahl hypothesis. As Professor J. D. Swales, head of the department of medicine at the Medical School at Leicester, explains:

> "Little fresh evidence was available but the medical climate had changed. Cardiovascular disease is the major health problem of Western society. The need to treat more and more otherwise healthy individuals with high blood pressure became frightening. The cost and the organisational problems posed by a life-time's drug treatment of up of 20 per cent of the adult population was seen as an appalling challenge. How much nicer if a simple change in habit could have the same effect ... The concept [of Dahl's hypothesis] was simple, it gripped the imagination and was easily

communicated." (39)

As a result, the Health Education Council bought full page advertisements in daily newspapers with the headline "What Shook 100 Million Americans into Eating Less Salt" (40). The Committee on Medical Aspects of Food Policy (COMA), set up by the DHSS, recommended that "the dietary intake of common salt should not be increased further and that consideration should be given to ways and means of decreasing it". (41)

Professor Swales comments:

> "The trouble is that the dietary scene includes a variety of experts with dubious credentials. Some are government-funded through the Health Education Council. Having at some stage accepted the case for salt restriction and having entered the public arena they find it difficult to turn back. The health educationist will be reassured in one respect even if the message changes. To misquote Harold Wilson, a year is a long time in health education. The healthy diet of milk, eggs and cheese of a few years back is now mercifully forgotten ... It is reasonable that society should protect its members, but protection surely does not extend to pretence and falsification." (42)

In 1984 13 experts from 8 different centres disputed the salt-hypertension link in The Lancet, and attacked the "evangelical crusade to present a simplistic view of the evidence that will prove attractive to the media." (43)

Hostile responses from the medical profession to challenges to the salt scare were largely emotional, in tone, rather than scientific. As Dr. Le Fanu has argued:

"[W]hen [its] protagonists are winkled out of their committee rooms to justify their position, we get affirmative rhetoric, emotional imagery, calls to solidarity. Everything, in short, except rationality. It is as if a religious belief had been challenged." (44)

7: The Fibre Furore

A book published in 1966 argued that the food eaten in the Western world was too refined, implying that in the refining process some desirable components – "fibres" – had been removed. It was the alleged absence of these components that accounted for the increased incidence of some diseases in the West, as compared with less industrialised countries. Although the book was thin on cause-and-effect data that were scientifically acceptable, a widespread belief emerged that the presence of fibre in food was beneficial, and that a great deal of food eaten in the West is too pure. In the words of Professor Ian Macdonald, head of the department of physiology at Guy's Hospital:

> "Because there is little in the way of fact, though it is increasing, there is an abundance of speculation on the role of dietary fibre in the prevention of disease, and some of the speculators display a fervour not often seen in science ... [T]he term dietary fibre means different things to different people, and an attempt has been made to accept a single definition of dietary fibre as 'the remnants of vegetable cell walls that are not hydrolysed by the alimentary enzymes of man' ... The high speculation-to-fact ratio in the field of dietary fibre could be reduced if careful research with fibre isolates could be carried out, preferably in man. Many of the preventative health claims made for dietary fibre may be true but it does a discredit to medicine and nutrition should any of these claims subsequently prove to be false." (45)

8: The Sugar Scam

In another alarmist book, *The Saccharine Disease*, by T. L. Cleave, it was argued that sugar and white flour in the diet were a major factor in causing such diseases as obesity, diabetes, diverticular disease and dental caries. Cleave did not consider sugar (sucrose) any more harmful than white flour, and the special emphasis on sugar as being supposedly harmful was emphasised by others. Yet there is no evidence to support the allegations that sugar is a cause of the diseases named by Cleave, and promoted by countless other books and articles with titles like Pure, White and Deadly.

In fact, sugar plays an important positive role in human health. According to G. Vettorazzi, a toxicologist:

> "Sugar, commonly known as table sugar, cane sugar, or beet sugar is one of the few organic compounds which play an important role in human nutrition, available in large quantities of high purity at a relatively low cost ... It is a compound toxicologically safe and nutritionally acceptable. Its direct intake in normal amounts should be recommendable as well as from excesses in nutrient intake." (46)

Barbara Rigg, writing in the magazine *New Health*, argued that sugar is a cause of hyperactivity, delinquency and criminal behaviour. But there is no scientific evidence to support this claim. Nor is there any such evidence to suggest that sugar consumption causes hypoglycemia (low blood sugar), which is alleged to be a cause of delinquent behaviour. In the United States, it is common for offenders to be compelled, as part of the rehabilitation process, to eat a diet low in sugar, despite the fact that no scientific evidence has ever demonstrated that diet causes or prevents criminal behaviour in an individual. Even the claim that sugar causes dental caries is a gross oversimplification. The prevalence of caries in children in Western countries has dramatically decreased over the past 20 years and is continuing to do so, although the per capita consumption of sugar and other carbohydrate has remained fairly constant, if anything slightly increasing. According to Marshall Midda, consultant dental surgeon and director of the school of dental hygiene at Bristol Dental Hospital:

> "[T]here is no current scientific basis for categorical statements concerning the potential relative carcinogenicity in humans of sugars or foods containing fermentable carbohydrates. It is frequency of carbohydrate consumption, rather than the amount of sugar consumed, which is the major dietary determinant of caries causation." (47)

In addition, the councils on dental health and health planning, dental research and dental therapeutics of the American Dental Association issued a joint statement on diet and caries, which declared:

> "Sucrose has traditionally been regarded as the carbohydrate most detrimental to teeth. Evidence indicates, however, that carcinogenic

bacteria can use other simple carbohydrates to produce acid in the mouth ... The Association recognises that the single action of decreasing total sucrose intake may be incomplete as a caries prevention measure. Many foods that contain little or no sucrose, but that do contain other fermentable carbohydrates are capable of promoting decay." (48)

Despite these facts, the myth of sugar being a harmful substance is still an article of faith among the health activists. As Professor Marks continues:

"Many people have been persuaded not only to deprive themselves – when it probably does not matter – but also children and sick people dependent upon them, of good wholesome foods containing sugar which they would enjoy and from which they would also benefit. We see this happening not only in the domestic situation but, even worse, in our public hospitals where misguided zealots insist upon feeding sick and elderly patients with bulky high-fibre food that they cannot or will not eat, whilst depriving them of palatable energy-rich food that they will, and which would provide them with the means of overcoming their illness."

(49)

The war against sugar continues, however. A survey of press coverage reveals stories like the following:

Michael Honsnell, "Dentist Strikes Off Children Who Eat Sweets", (*The Times*, 27 June, 1994, p. 1)

"My Son Was Sugar addict, Says [Eric] Clapton. Tragic Conor's Craving".

"'I didn't think he should be drinking Coca Cola. I didn't think it was good for him,'
'That's when I first encountered a full-tilt tantrum, ... He lay on the floor and screamed for what seemed like hours. Real hysterics, as if he was in a withdrawal situation. It was sugar addiction."' (*The Daily Express*, 25 February 1992, p. 7)

"Coke Banned From Schools"

"Soft drinks, including Coca Cola and Pepsi Cola, are to banned from

sale in Singapore schools. The aim is to reduce obesity among students."
(*The Evening Standard*, 22 April, 1992)

There is, of course, a state funded pressure group like ASH, "Action and Information on Sugar" (AIS), that spreads alarmist stories and pressurises the government to enact coercive paternalism and censorship. One of its principal themes is, as is to be expected, the protection of "children and young people". The sale of "sugary" sports drinks "and their promotion to the public, particularly young people" is thus singled out. (See Sue Dibb, "Sweeter Side of an Athlete's Diet", *The Times*, 25 September 1992. Dibb is not an independent journalist, but an activist for the alarmist group the National Food Alliance, of which more anon).

And like all health fascist groups AIS wants to censor any alternative views on their subject matter. It thus campaigns for the "screening" of publicity and educational material on sugar from the trade body the Sugar Board or other sources ("Resources: 1: Propaganda Good and Bad; Resources II: Sugar Wars", *The Guardian*, 26 November 1991).

Various products are singled out for alarmist, and sometimes silly, attacks. Thus, it complained to the Advertising Standards Authority that the slogan "A Mars a day helps you work, rest and play" was scientifically misleading – a claim thankfully rejected by the ASA ("A Mars a Day Keeps the Food Campaigners at Bay", *The Guardian*, 20 June 1992). But the protection of children remains the most fruitful ploy. Three new bedtime chocolate drinks were thus attacked, and the press duly obliged with headlines like:

"New Drinks for Babies 'Rot Teeth'." (*The Daily Telegraph*, 9 November 1992)

"Wiping the Smiles Off Young Faces". (*The Times*, 25 November 1993, p. 17)

The political exploitation of children is especially marked in another ploy of the anti-sugar campaign, that of alarmism regarding childrens' drinks. Like the anti-smokers, who create fronts which are allegedly "childrens initiatives", action taken by politically and ideologically motivated adults is described as that of children. Legal attempts to blame manufacturers for what tooth decay, which, if it did have any connection with the use of their drinks, would be as a result of inappropriate use or neglect of dental hygiene by the parents is thus described by the press in the following terms:

Lawyers are acting "for children" in legal action against the manufacturers of baby drinks, including Ribena, Boots, and Cow & Gate, claiming that "products give unsufficient warning about the dangers of tooth decay resulting from prolonged contact with sugary drinks" ("Parenting", *Spare Rib*, No. 238, Octone/November 1992, p. 65)

"1,200 children have joined a group action, "Infant Drinks Litigation Group". ("Baby Drink Makers to be Sued Over Sugar", *The Times*, 20 April 1994, p. 7) (50)

9: The Coffee Campaign

Amazingly, even coffee has been portrayed as a threat to life as we know it:

"Coffee Boosts Danger of Death by Heart Disease." (*The Independent*, 17 October 1986)

"Peril in the Percolator?" (*The Daily Express*, 17 October 1986)

Dr. Vernon Coleman, "Are You Hooked on Your Cuppa?" (*The Daily Star*, 4 December 1986)

"Coffee Perk."

"Dependence on coffee is one of the most common of minor vices despite its well-known side- effects, such as irritability, insomnia, tremor, irregular heart action and the irritable bowel syndrome." (*The Times*, 22 February, 1989)

"Pick-me-up is a let down".

"Coffee us widely regarded as a reliable ally by those seeking a pick-me-up. But it does not always have the desired effect. In fact, it can pack a powerful tranquillising punch – leaving people tired and groggy. This knock-me-down reaction is uncommon, but nonetheless affects thousands of people. The American Journal of Medicine has reported seven such cases ... They are also warning people that excess caffeine intake can put people at risk from heart disease." (*The Guardian*, 22 June 1990)

"Caffeine Dependence Syndrome"

"[C]affeine exhibits the features of a typical psychoactive substance of dependence. It is valuable to recognise caffeine dependence as a clinical syndrome ... " (Eric C. Strain et al, "Caffeine Dependence Syndrome: Evidence From Case Histories and Experimental Evaluations", *Journal of the American Medical Association*, 272(13), 5 October, 1994, pp. 1043)

Jill Palmer, "Can Coffee Give You Cancer?" (*The Daily Mirror*, 2 March 1995, p. 6)

"Coffee Linked With Diabetes in Babies"

"Pregnant women who are heavy coffee drinkers may be giving their unborn children diabetes, a study published today suggests. Researchers from Finland and America are pointing to a strong statistical correlation between countries with high coffee consumption and those with high levels of insulin-dependent diabetes, the type that usually affects young people." (*The Guardian*, 9th March 1990)

Douglas Skrecky, "drug Addiction: Notes on Caffeine, Chelation and Melatonin",

"The age of acceptance of nicotine is past, but there is another drug which still commands respect ... CAFFEINE... this drug is far from being innocuous. It is probably the greatest cause of unnecessary human suffering in the western hemisphere". (*Longeveity Report*, No. 45, June 1993, p. 17)

In 1990 a London local radio station announced a news item with the words, " 'Too much coffee can put you in a straight-jacket', says Consultant Psychiatrist." When he was interviewed, the psychiatrist in fact said that the drinking of four or more cups of coffee could make one "anxious, rude or possibly aggressive". This is a particularly telling example of how the media grossly exaggerates health claims.

In reality, it has been known for at least 150 years that all caffeinated beverages can cause a variety of subjective symptoms and objective changes in behaviour when they are taken in excess. Yet these signs and symptoms can also result from a variety of conditions such as thyrotoxicosis, pheochromocytoma and anxiety neurosis. Many people who believe themselves to be sensitive to the pharmacological effects of caffeine turn out not to be so when tested double blind. Professor Marks thus reports that:

"Only a very few cases of genuine caffeine intoxication have come to light from amongst the many hundreds and possibly thousands of people that my colleagues and I have tested over the years, even when caffeine intoxication was strongly suspected clinically. For the vast majority of people, caffeinated beverages are perfectly safe ... Caffeine does not, for example, cause cancer, high blood pressure of fetal abnormalities, all of which have been laid at its door at some time or another and shown to be false. But when have dull old facts been allowed to stand in the way of exciting new myths – especially in the writing of popular articles on the dangers of food and drink?" (51)

10: Listeriosis and Salmonella Scares

Listeriosis was a comparatively minor food scare which first came to popular attention in the United States in 1985, and received widespread media coverage in Britain in 1987. It has long been known to medical practitioners, as an uncommon and sporadic infectious disease confined almost entirely to pregnant women and their fetuses, newborn babies, the elderly and people suffering from diseases which weaken the body's immune system. The agent that causes listeriosis is any one of a large number of strains of listeria monocytogenes, a widespread bacteria found in many foods. Following an outbreak in California in 1985, compulsory reporting of listeriosis was introduced in that state for the first time anywhere in the world. It emerged that listeriosis occurred with a frequency of

12 cases per million of the population per year, and almost all the reported cases had occurred in subjects known to be susceptible. There is no common pattern of infectivity, nor any reason to believe that listeriosis is any more common now than it was in the past. Better recognition, however, has led to more frequent diagnosis.

Bacteria of the genus Salmonella cause many diseases, including typhoid and paratyphoid fevers, both of which are fatal and spread by drinking contaminated water. Other types of Salmonella cause food poisoning, which is associated with mass catering, especially when it involves poultry dishes. Thorough cooking of food containing Salmonella organisms renders it sterile, and most outbreaks of food poisoning caused by Salmonella are due to poor hygiene in the preparation or storage of food, especially poultry. It has long been recognised that eggs may be a source of salmonellosis although it was thought that this was always due to microorganisms on the outer shell getting into the egg or the cook's hands during preparation, followed by insufficient cooking which failed to kill all the organisms.

In 1988, the idea first emerged that eggs with unbroken shells might themselves both contain Salmonella and do so in sufficient numbers to cause illness in somebody eating them. In Britain it led to one of the longest and most expensive food scares in history, culminating in the resignation of Edwina Currie, MP, as junior health minister. As Professor Marks comments, "The grounds upon which the scandal was based, namely that eating eggs that had not been hardboiled constituted a real hazard to health, was grossly exaggerated. Indeed, the evidence that food poisoning has ever been caused by eating soft-boiled eggs or even raw ones for that matter, is anecdotal at best and based upon laboratory observations that a small proportion of eggs produced by hens infected with Salmonella become infected before the shell is fully formed whilst still in the hen's body. Perhaps the reason that this happening does not cause more problems is that infected hens also produce antibodies which they secrete into the eggs and probably prevent the bacteria from multiplying." (52)

The announcement by Junior Health Minister Edwina Currie in

December 1988 that "most of the egg production in [Britain] ... is now infected with salmonella", created a devastating slump in egg sales and a field day for alarmists and for the deployment of "creative" statistics. Dr. Le Fanu discussed an "elite confidential document from a dreary and anonymous committee. This estimates two million cases of salmonella each year".

But how he asked, was this figure arrived at?

> "They take", he revealed, "the 24,000 reported cases last year. Multiplied the number by 100 because of the problem of under-reporting and – hey presto – we get to more than two million.

> But why multiply it by 100, why not 10 or even 1,000. All the figures arrived at by this method of computation have only one thing in common – they are as meaningless as Edwina's original observations on the matter"

Meanwhile the bacteriologists are feverishly analysing tens of thousands of eggs to find the culprit for this supposed pandemic – and are lucky to find one that is contaminated.

Then there is listeria in, among other foods, soft cheese. An 'expert' announced on Friday that half of the pregnant women who contracted listeria lost their babies. But how can he tell? No scientist has been culturing the remnants of miscarriages to find the evidence of the organism. Nor indeed is there any way of ascertaining who the remaining 50 per cent of pregnant women might be who allegedly get infected and don't lose their babies." (53)

Richard North and Teresa Gorman's IEA Health and Welfare Unit Paper *Chickengate: An Independent Analysis of the Salmonella in Eggs Scare* (54). They conclusively demonstrate that there was no evidence to blame eggs for the initial alleged 49 outbreaks of food poisoning which precipitated the crisis, and that good scientific reasons existed to doubt the existence of an "epidemic" of salmonella poisoning and the role of eggs in any real food poisoning cases. Unfortunately, legal constraints prevented the authors revealing all about the behind-the-scenes stratagems that resulted in the Currie Scare. What is clear is that, as they put it, the investigation of food poisoning had fallen into a "morass of pseudo-science and ideological zeal." (55)

The Currie Debacle, however, as Richard North has argued elsewhere, led to two "quite separate regulatory disasters".

The first and more localised were the immediate consequences for the egg industry when, to "restore consumer confidence" in eggs, the Ministry of Agriculture introduced compulsory slaughter for all poultry flocks found to be infected. As North puts it:

> "About 3.5 million birds were killed and thousands of chicken farmers went out of business – until in February [1993] a report chaired by microbiologist Heather Dick confirmed what many veterinary scientists had warned all along: scientifically the policy was totally misconceived. Having caused immense damage since it was introduced in 1989, it was immediately abandoned."

However, a much wider disaster followed, when, in North's words:

> ... to show that it was 'doing something' about food poisoning, the Government introduced the Food Safety Act, giving draconian powers to environmental health officers. This has led to an unprecedented 'hygiene blitz' affecting half a million food-handling operations from shops, restaurants and hotels, to clubs, schools, canteens and old peoples homes.

The cost of 'improvements' has run into billions of pounds. Thousands of businesses have closed because they are unable to afford to comply with new requirements. And a nearly universal complaint has been the confrontational attitude of often young, inexperienced [Environmental Health Officers], who seem unable to demonstrate a practical eye for genuine hygiene risks." (56)

Combined with the growing inroads of EEC bureaucratic regulation in Britain food fascism has played its part in the broader phenomenon of what North and Christopher Booker have called *The Mad Officials*, in their book of that name: a massive proliferation of frequently insane regulation of business enterprise, malicious and destructive, and the destruction of the livelihoods of countless individuals. (57)

And the food fascists continue their mendacious propaganda. In May of 1994 People for the Ethical Treatment of Animals (PETA) launched "its first major offensive in the UK against the meat industry". In its "Chicken Out", campaign it repeated the misleading claims about salmonella, stressed the "dangers of eating chicken", the alleged dangers of its high cholesterol content, and the fact that "tons of manure from the industry seriously pollutes the environment". (58) And as of writing, the Vegetarian Society has just launched a hysterical poster and publicity campaign against meat in general.

11: Mad Cow Disease (BSE)

Bovine Spongiform Encephalopathy is a new disease in cows which was first reported to the Ministry of Agriculture, Fisheries and Food in 1986. In 1990 it received a great deal of media attention under the nickname "mad cow disease". A diagnosis of BSE in a cow depends upon the presence of characteristic neuropathological features which are discovered only at post- mortem, features similar to those seen in a number of other diseases which occur in man and animals. In 1976, Gajdusek was awarded the Nobel Prize for physiology and medicine for discovering that these features are caused by transmissible agents which differ from all other types of transmissible agents such as parasites, bacteria and virus-causing diseases. These agents are called 'prions'. They are resistant to inactivation by physical and chemical agents (such as heat) which destroy normal bacteria and do not provoke the normal immunological reactions (such as the production of antibodies) which normally neutralise the effect of extraneous organisms and toxins on the body. There has never been a case in which BSE has been transmitted to a human being from any other species, and as Professor Marks comments, "as far as we know it cannot be transmitted to man from any other species. Just as human beings do not seem to be susceptible to the virus that to be susceptible to the causative agent of BSE, whatever it may be ... [T]he risk of acquiring BSE from eating meat from healthy cows would seem to be so small as to be insignificant." (59)

Unfortunately this one has run and run, and is still running. But the truth of the matter is, as Dr. Michael Apple declared, that "more people will probably be injured, inconvenienced or killed as a result of travelling to all the conferences, committees and seminars that will be spawned by the mad cow scare than will die from the disease itself after the next 20 years". (60)

12: Irradiation of Food

It is ironic, but utterly predictable, that the food fascists should be equally hysterical about one of this century's scientific innovations to ensure increased food safety: gamma irradiation. Irradiation is a method of rendering organic matter sterile without altering its physical or chemical nature. Professor Marks comments on these scares:

> "It is only by extrapolating far beyond data, implying guilt by association rather than on evidence and by fostering people's confusion between irradiation of food and radioactivity in food – which was highlighted by the Chernobyl disaster – that the scare mongers have been able to delude the people and even the Government into believing that food irradiation is harmful and should be banned. Fortunately the Government has recently seen sense and intends to permit regulated irradiation of food." (61)

In America, a group called "Food and Water", has sent threatening letters to food industry executives, warning darkly of the "carcinogenic risks" of irradiation, and threatening smear campaigns against treated foods. The hysteria of such campaigns, feeding on false associations with nuclear radioactivity, has delayed the introduction of this beneficial technology. (62) In Britain, the National Food Alliance (of which more anon, below) has promoted the scare against food irradiation.

14: The War against McDonalds

Virtually all of the themes of food fascism can be found in what has become a symbolic issue for the movement: the war against McDonalds.

"Starving the Poor ... Destroying the Earth ... Ruining Your Health ... Murdering Animals ... Exploiting Their Staff". These are the subheadings of a leaflet distributed by a group called "Greenpeace London" (not actually a part of the official Greenpeace organisation) which is now the subject of a current libel action by McDonalds against its principal writers and distributors. The latter, of course, like to portray themselves as being in a "David and Goliath" like contest with a giant and "powerful" corporation, and much press coverage of the case is slanted against the company. But the reality of the issues is that the only "power" McDonald's has is that of offering a product to consumers who make the free decision to purchase it. The outrageous smears and lies of the anti-McDonald's movement is precisely calculated to destroy McDonalds by defaming their product and reputation.

The viciousness of the campaign is striking: "McBastards" (63), "McLiers, McTorturers, McCancer" (64), and "eco-fouling burger-mongers" (65), are typical headlines and phrases in *Labour Briefing* and other socialist publications on the subject. (66)

The claims of the campaign are the usual mixture of half-truths, outright lies and contentious interpretations. In fact, the accusations made against McDonalds could be equally aimed at any business. They are based upon extreme environmentalist claims, for example, regarding the "rain forests" and "global warming", upon assumptions that any form of manufacture which uses natural resources and produces waste is wicked, that raising and eating animals is wicked, that providing employment at market rates is "exploitation", and that a company has no right not to recognise trade unions. Indeed, it is clear that McDonald's is being singled out in an attempt to "[make] people aware of the exploitation of workers, animals and nature involved in the production of commodities by transnational corporations like McDonalds" (67). Labour MP Jeremy Corbyn has also used his Parliamentary privilege to repeat the libels against McDonalds.

The campaign against McDonalds has involved violent attacks by socialist rioters in Copenhagen, who quite explicitly declared as their reason that it "symbolises capitalism and money". In Wellington, New Zealand on "UN World Food Day", demonstrators put a mock "Ronald MacDonald" (the McDonald's clown-like promotional figure) in stocks outside their largest branch. Campaigners have even managed to propagandise a former "Ronald McDonald" actor, one Geoff Guliana, who has now apologised to the peoples of the world "for brainwashing children". (68)

Elsewhere, groups of socialist and Marxist activists frequently organise to prevent the opening of new branches. The combination of upper class snobbery and socialist distaste for a commercial enterprise serving ordinary working people a reasonably priced product, was particularly amusing when the local socialist intelligentsia, including Michael Foot, campaigned to prevent the intrusion of such a plebeian intrusion into their refined area. But even in the tatty, dilapidated, mugger-prone, condom and needle-strewn wastelands of Kings Cross, the "left" campaigned against the establishment of a McDonalds in the area. "You're Not Welcome Here", shouted Alan Beale of the local Marxist/Socialist Anarchist/Pacifist bookshop Housemans, at a demonstration at the opening of the branch. And the local council also tried to blackmail McDonald's into funding and granting other benefits to local "charities" (i.e., politicised pressure groups) in exchange for planning permission for their branch. (69)

15: The Real Politics of Food

It should be clear that the political "left", increasingly defeated and discredited in the realms of political and economic thought and policy, are attempting to establish a new ideological hegemony in the discourse of diet and heath. The real sub-text of that discourse is one of fear, hysteria, technophobia, and anti-capitalism. And their goal, of course, is to establish themselves as the "saviours" of the masses now threatened by the wicked barons of food – a deliverance from danger which, unsurprisingly, seems to entail placing them in positions of power and authority and replacing free choice and liberty by state dictation and paternalism.

The medical establishment, especially in Britain and America, is now overwhelmingly committed to coercive "preventive medicine", and to the extension of health fascism from its focus on smoking to that of obesity and other allegedly food-related illness. The former US Surgeon General has thus claimed that "obesity related conditions are the second-leading cause of death in the US, resulting in about 300, 000 lives lost each year", and called for a national policy to deal with this "problem". (70) Dr. William Dietz, Director of Clinical Nutrition at New England Medical Centre in Boston, similarly denounced the fact that "There is no commitment to obesity as a public health problem" in America, whilst the Chairwoman of New York University's Department of Nutrition Chairwoman deplores the fact that "Advertising budgets for food that no one needs are astronomical", and that people are "constantly bombarded with food messages that encourage them to eat more than they need". (71).

In Britain Sir Richard Doll, not content with his central role in the anti-smoking campaign, claims that 30% of cancer cases and perhaps half of heart disease could be avoided by dietary change. He thus calls for a "food policy". (72)

Like the anti-smoking movement, food fascism has its lobby groups, similarly subsidised by ample infusions of tax-payers money. The central groups are the National Food Alliance (NFA) and the Food Commission.

i: The National Food Alliance

The National Food Alliance is headed by one Geoffrey Cannon, author of *The Politics of Food* and co-author, with Caroline Walker, of *The Food Scandal*.

The propaganda themes of Canon and the NFA are tediously predicable. The prime target is advertising, especially "food advertising on television to children" and "advertisers, keen to push any product with big budgets .. and manufacturers who, like the tobacco industry are focussing on young, impressionable people at the time when lifelong habits are formed" (73).

Of course, Mr. Cannon thinks it quite alright to focus his propaganda on "young, impressionable people", and prevent them via censorship from hearing any viewpoint other than his.

Anyone who disagrees with Mr. Canon is smeared as having mercenary motives and defamed as "hirelings" (74) of the wicked capitalists. Canon's constant comparisons of his against the food industry with the struggle against tobacco is significant, and repeatedly proves himself a master of defamation. When writers in Marketing Magazine dared to criticise his campaign Canon labelled such criticism as "swivel-eyed paranoia" and once again compared them to the tobacco industry, who, he claimed. "slander(ed) those working in the public interest". And since only the wicked could obviously oppose "the public interest" (i.e., health fascists like himself and the anti-smoking movement), any criticism obviously comes from "pseudo-independent" groups he claims are "set up" by the tobacco industry. Precisely what slanders the tobacco industry was supposed to have enunciated Mr. Canon never specified. His were, and always are, rather obvious. (75)

The National Food Alliance is supported by, and works with and through, a huge network of similarly authoritarian and paternalist groups, ranging from the pro-Marxist Catholic Institute for International Relations, Friends of the Earth, the Green Alliance, the Coronary Protection Group, Action & Information on Sugars, the Food Additives Campaign Team, Baby Milk Action, Parents for Safe Food, as well as the Bakers, Food and Allied Workers Union and so on.

Their campaign against food advertising resulted in persuading the Independent Television Commission (ITC) in February 1995 to set up a new code of standards concentrating on preventing children from picking up unhealthy eating habits. The code established rules which (similar to the "voluntary" (sic) rules on tobacco adverting) banned jokes about healthy diets, showing people eating late at night, or buying large quantities of sweets. "There was concern that children might not clean their teeth afterwards". No longer would civilisation be threatened by the ad showing Harry Enfield "packing a shopping trolley with Dime bars (it could have provoked gluttony" (76). (Interestingly, the rules also restricted the times when alcohol can be advertised and placed limitations on mentioning speed in car advertising, other areas of concern to health fascists, safety nazis and growing anti-car movement)

As with the anti-smoking movement, though, such restrictions are never enough. A total ban is their real goal. The NFA's Sue Dibbs declared that the guidelines "failed to, address the cumulative message to children – a message that overwhelmingly portrays fatty and sugary foods as attractive and desirable food choices" (77).

In 1993 the NFA issued its *Children: Advertisers Dream, Nutrition Nightmare* Report, coinciding with (and obviously meant to reinforce) the publication of the Nutrition Task Force's Draft programme. Like the same sort of literature produced by the anti-smoking lobby on tobacco advertising, although dressed up in the trappings of scholarship, the Report ignored the modern scholarship on the economics of advertising, the real sociology of consumption, and ignored important distinctions between mature and growing markets. The Advertising Association commissioned an independent study by Patrick Barwise, Professor of Management at the London Business School, who concluded that "the quality of the NFA report's analysis is so poor that its actual contribution to knowledge and understanding is very limited". Independent researcher Caroline Sharp also found that many of the Report's references either did not in reality support the argument or were references to the lobby group's own previous work! (78)

Needless to say, the NFA has never responded to such criticisms, and merely recycles it claims in further reports like *Easy to Swallow, Hard to Stomach*, which called for complete bans of television advertisements for fatty and sugary foods at times when large numbers of children are watching. The Advertising Association has also demonstrated how NFA questions added to MORI's Omnibus survey in June of 1994 were loaded, and their interpretation of the results equally contentious. (79)

Occasionally a note of criticism does enter into press coverage of the NFA demands. "What I find hard to stomach", wrote Tom Kemp in *The Daily Telegraph*, "was the claim by the alliance's spokeswoman, Sue Dibb, that she was concerned that [food] ads undermined parental authority. Rubbish! The whole health lobby is part of a massive conspiracy to undermine parental authority ... What really annoys the National Food Alliance and every other or organisation devoted to making us live healthier lives, whether we like it or not, is that ads for sweets and ice-lollies undermine their authority. They do this by giving children a glimpse of the delights they could enjoy the free world beyond the Reich of lentils and muesli." (80)

Indeed!

Another central part of the NFA strategy, again similar to the anti-smoking movement, is to infiltrate a government body, inquiry or report to ensure that it espouses their partisan viewpoint. Should say, a report then be challenged, within or without the government, it can then be revealed in tones of scandal that a "cover-up" is going on at the behest of "vested interests" and their "hirelings" determined to destroy the health of the nation for mere profit

A successful example of this strategy was the Nutrition Task Force (NTF), one of the many such groups set up by the government to help achieve the targets of its obnoxious "Health of the Nation" plan. The NTF was dominated by NFA supporters and provided a major input into the Committee on Medical Aspects of Food Policy (COMA) recommendations on diet: urging people to reduce their intake of salt by a third, to eat at least two portions of fish per week, to increase bread, potato, fruit and vegetable consumption by a third, and to take more physical exercise.

The resulting Daily Telegraph headline and coverage was typical:

"Damning Health Report 'Withheld', Alarm Over Huge Rise in Obesity"

"An expert report predicting an explosion in obesity that could lead to a disastrous decline in general health has been withheld by ministers for three months. Whitehall sources say the report, which predicts that by the year 2005 a quarter of British women and 18 percent of men will be obese, has been delayed because of lobbying by vested interests and because of its far-reaching repercussions" (*The Daily Telegraph*, September 30, 1995)

What is particularly galling in all this is the bare-faced cheek of the health fascist in denying there is anything coercive in their proposals! One of their apologists, Judy Jones, writing in The Observer, replying to the criticism of the report as an example of nanny state paternalism thus declared: "It's not about telling people what to do and banning cream cakes. If people don't know, they don't have to listen". She twists reality by accusing the critics of the report of trying to suppress free speech: "What right have they got to stop the rest of us finding out how to eat healthily if we want to". And, predictably, she defames the critics:

"At the heart of all this hysterical and spurious nonsense, spouted in the name of individual freedom, is the rather more pertinent freedom of the food giants to make millions selling sugary, fatty, additive-rich confections to an ill-informed, confused public". (81)

Similarly, Professor Michael Marmot, head of epidemiology and public health at University College, London, and Chairman of the COMA, also claimed that: "We are not telling people what to do".

This from a man whose report was indeed telling people what to do, and even endorsed extreme social engineering in the form of town planning aimed at decreasing car usage and forcing people to walk or cycle more!

Marmot similarly attacked his critics as "commercial interests" and misrepresented the existence of scientific disagreement by claiming that: "You have to look at science and look at whom is making the statements. It is often hard to hear what they are saying over the deafening din of grinding axes". (82)

That claims to have no agenda of coercion are utterly ingenuous was further demonstrated by the comments of Professor Philip James, Director of Rowett Research Institute in Aberdeen, President of the NFA, and a member of the Nutrition Task Force. He was full of praise for policies in Norway and Finland, where "a coherent health strategy that has permeated every aspect of everyday life". (83)

It is surely not calling a spade a bloody shovel to identify the policies favoured by the NFA and the other food fascists as a massive politicisation of society in the name of health. A "coherent strategy ... permeat[ing] every aspect of everyday life" is simply "healthspeak" for totalitarian social engineering – but all for our own good, of course.

Since virtually every academic or scholar working in the field of nutrition or other food related issues has some sort of contact with the food industry, the tactic of smearing them as mercenary pawns of the "food barons" is easy. An ongoing attempt to discredit any critic of the food fascists by "revealing" his industry links should thus be expected. (84)

ii: The Food Commission

What is now called the Food Commission was originally set up as the London Food Commission in April 1983, one of the many Marxist and socialist groups funded by rate-payers money by the Greater London Council under "Red" Ken Livingstone.

It described itself as "in a position relative to the food industry as ASH is to the tobacco world", and its assumptions were a mixture of traditional Marxist ones and health fascism. Food choices, for example, were in their view not made freely by consumers, but by "just five major retailers". They claimed that it cost the National Health Service £1000 million for treating allegedly dietary related diseases. And concern was expressed at advertisements "aimed directly and indirectly at women". (The poor little things get so easily confused and misled, you see). Part time and "low paid" work for women in food industry was also raised as an issue of concern. (85)

Tim Lang, Director of London Food Commission, eventually moved to become head of "Parents for Safe Food" (PSF), a group affiliated to the NFA, an indeed, a Trustee of it. (86) PSF was founded by comiediene Pamela Stephenson, to campaign against Alar, a pesticide used on fruit, especially apples. Ms. Stephenson and Mr. Lang were apparently proud of this campaign, although it was subsequently found to be entirely baseless. Even the WHO and the American National Academy of Sciences, repudiated the scare. (87) An auspicious start, and perhaps indicative of how much confidence can be placed in the Food Commission and its supporters.

Lang is author of *The Safe Food Book*, and has also worked with the (so-called) Catholic Institute of International Relations, an organisation noted for consistently supporting Marxist causes and policies which have been disastrous for the freedom and prosperity of the masses. They have both opposed free trade. (88), which Lang speaks about in terms of "pillaging the world in consumer and production terms" (89)

Typical of the Commission's anti-capitalism was the imagery it employed in "This Food Business", a supplement produced jointly with the socialist weekly *The New Statesman* to accompany a Channel 4 television series: a picture of an apple penetrated by a maggot whose trail draws a pound sign! (90)

Themes championed by the Food Commission especially include the alleged dangers of food additives, and, of course, their special danger to children. The press dutifully rewards their propaganda with headlines like:

"Snack Makers Use Additives Children Should Not Eat." (*The Times*, 26 April 1993)

"After Dinner, How About Some Chewing Gum?"

"[T]he Food Commission says that chewing gum contains 'secret' ingredients that may add up to a potent cocktail of toxic chemicals. The mineral hydrocarbons used in the gum base, such as Vaseline and paraffin wax, are known to cause tumours in experimental animals. The commission says that if the gum is chewed in conjunction with fatty foods, such as chocolate, the hydrocarbons may be leached out of the gum and released into the stomach". (*The Independent*, 15 January 1991)

Advertising, is of course, a bogey. According to the Commissions Tim Lobstein, it "gets more sophisticated and compelling". Censorship is necessary to "protect the health of the nation's young." (91)

And even when manufacturers do make allegedly "health" low-fat foods, they are gouging them with excessive profits and "discouraging consumers from eating a healthier diet by charging up to 40 percent more for low-fat versions of their products". (92)

iii: The Lancet

Interesting light on the real politics of food can be shed by examining the views of the former Editor of The *Lancet*, Ian Munro, who consistently championed food fascism (His editorship ending at the beginning of this decade). Munro was outspoken in denouncing the "unscrupulous profit motive antagonistic to health – interests of, principally, the pharmaceutical, tobacco, alcohol and food industries". Munro was also involved with International Physicians for the Prevention of Nuclear War, a so called "peace" group, but in reality a Soviet front group which consistently championed policies favoured by Soviet totalitarianism and opposed effective Western defence against the horrors of that system. He also peddled a piece of propagandistic pseudo-science favoured by other Soviet fellow-travellers. This was the nonsense that there was a serious "psychological problem" emerging in children throughout the western world: "a fear of a nuclear holocaust casting a long and pessimistic shadow over their hopes for the future". (93) In fact, Munro was an active member of the Communist Party of Great Britain – in other words a supporter of a system of tyranny responsible for more misery and death than even the German National Socialists.

iv: Other Groups

The manufacture of food scares is certainly not confined to the NFA and Food Commission, however. An incestuous network of inter-related individuals, groups and campaigns can be relied upon to deliver a constant stream of alarms and policy demands. Thus, the National Consumer Council called for a "food charter" for consumers. (94) The Consumers Association is often believed to be independent and objective, but somehow it almost always supports statist policies and alarmist propaganda. It is also a member of the NFA, and thus adds its two-h'pen'worth of alarmism:

"Restaurant Eating 'A Health Gamble'."

"Restaurants which serve dishes laden with excess fat are turning eating out into a 'health gamble', says the Consumers' Association Good Food Guide 1990." (*The Daily Telegraph*, 19 October, 1989)

The Coronary Prevention Group (CPG) and National Forum for Coronary Heart Disease Prevention (NFCHD), both member of the NFA, similarly issue a stream of scares and political demands.

Thus, the NFCHD, in March 1994, issued *Food for Children: Influencing Choice and Investing in Health*, which claimed that children in Britain were suffering from increasing undernourishment, demanded restrictions on food advertisements, the removal of vending machines from schools, and an end to school meals based on burgers, sausages and chips. (95)

Whilst the CPG claimed that:

"Up to 500 people a week are dying prematurely from heart attacks because the public is denied the nutrition information already required on pet food labels, health campaigners for the Coronary Prevention Group claimed yesterday ... deaths [could] be avoided if everyone used explicit packet warnings to help them tailor their diets to the lower fat and sugar guidelines recommended by the Department of Health." (96)

The truth of this claim can be judged in the light of the reality that more than 300 risk factors have been discovered to affect heart disease. How can the CPG decide which of these have the most effect? The total of deaths from all kinds of heart disease in England and Wales between birth and 64 years is, according to the Office of Population Censuses and Surveys, 32,439. Anti-smoking campaigners claim most of these for smoking! There isn't, if we take out the 26,000 demanded by the CPG, very many left for the other 300 risk factors. Moreover, none of these take into account recent research on the role in heart disease of the Heliocobacter pylori, a childhood acquired bacterial infection – which obviously cannot be shown to have any connection with eating habits, or, indeed, smoking.

The CPG's Director Michael O'Connor has made repeated anti-capitalist remarks, denouncing profit and calling for legal controls over advertisements (97)

The CPG is also particularly concerned to ensure that competing viewpoints are suppressed. In 1992 it published a discussion document (with participation by the Health Education Council and the National Consumer Council), advocating "detailed guidelines and an accreditation scheme to raise the standard of ... material on health and food". In other words, censorship of material that contradicts their views. Such censorship was justified in the usual emotionalistic (and insultingly sexist) terms of protecting women and children. Our heartstrings are pulled by images of "desperate mothers ... particularly vulnerable to advertising dressed up as health education", of "soft targets, including school children and patients at general clinics and doctor's surgeries." (98)

The food fascists also enjoy a highly privileged role in the media. BBC Radio 4's "The Food Programme" is virtually their house organ, with Derek Cooper fond of smears at "Thatcherism" and questioning the integrity of researchers who take a different view. The programme champions every scare and trumpets every demand for increased regulations and paternalism.

15: The Continuity of Food Fascism

The audacity of the claims of contemporary food fascists that they are "not telling people what to do", is also underlined by their clear admiration, and ill-concealed desire, to return to a state-dictated form of diet like war-time rationing. Indeed, there seems to be an almost direct ideological continuity from older statists like Labour politician Douglas Jay, who, in 1947 declared that "in the case of nutrition and health ... the gentleman in Whitehall really does know better what is good for the people than the people themselves". (99)

Earlier academic defenders of dietary statism could also be found. Typical were J. C. Drummond and Anne Wilbraham, authors of *The Englishman's Food: A History of Five Centuries of English Diet.* (100) These authors presented the disproved interpretation of the Industrial Revolution as a period of decline in living standards for the masses with an ill- concealed lust for a return to war-time dietary controls: "Much was accomplished during the Second World War when, owing to rationing and control, it was difficult to obtain an ill-balanced diet". (101)

That admiration for rationing remains unabashed, as much as their apologists will deny it public. Sheilah Bingham, reviewing the Medical Research Councils recommendations for reaching *Health of the Nation* targets in *The British Medical Journal*, clearly regrets that food rationing and taxes on fatty foods" are probably "politically unacceptable".

Professor Peter Boyle, head of epidemiology at the European Institute of Oncology in Milan, is also full of praise for the ration-imposed war-time diet. "For the first time there was a sys-

tematic attempt to make sure everybody enjoyed a balance diet"
(102)

"During the second world war we had a responsible government
providing its people with a healthy diet", declared another apologist
for health fascism, who also opined that "Food is being tampered
with by faceless people for profit." (103) And Colin Spencer, writing
in *The Guardian*, attacked "Thatcherism" in favour of the
paternalism of "old style Tories [who] were good in this role" of
dictating to the masses for their own good. In Spencer's view it was
the role of government to "encourage its citizens" and to "stimulate
and suppress demand by price control". (104)

16: Political Vegetarianism

At its even more extreme end food fascism becomes a form of
politicised vegetarianism imbued with anti-capitalist, technophobic
anti-industrialism. Such political vegetarians thus campaign for the
removal of meat, dairy products, fats and all animal products from
government dietary guidelines. (105) Such vegetarianism bases itself
upon not merely tendentious claims about the health benefits of
abstaining from meat – "Meat Eaters Die Before Vegetarians", as
one press headline put it (106) – but equally tendentious claims
about agriculture and economics. Thus, as Labour MP Tony Banks
claims:

> "Millions of people the world over are dying of starvation but 38% of all
> crops are fed to animals, so as to produce meat, most of which is
> consumed in the industrialised countries". (107)

Political vegetarianism has also become part of fashionable "PC"
posing, and we thus witness the invasion of the self-righteous
"celebrity vegetarian". During the Wings tour of the USA in 1991,
Paul and Linda McCartney, notorious examples of the worst
sanctimonious and priggish attitudes, would only pay for meals for
band members if they were vegetarian ones. Madonna fired a
member of one of her production crews for eating meat, whilst
"radical" playwright G. F. Newman, banned meat on the set of one

his BBC television productions. So blinded by self-righteousness and their mission to impose dietary correctness upon others are such vegetarians that they are unable even to recognise the nature of their actions. "He wasn't imposing his beliefs", claimed a vegetarian spokesperson about the Newman case. "If you feel very strongly about meat-eating it can be offensive to see someone else doing it, just as an asthmatic would feel strongly about someone smoking in their presence" (108).

Political vegetarianism is a systematic ideological attack upon free market economics, its assumptions just rehashed Marxism, with some of the old players (the proletariat, alienation, increasing immiseration, monopoly capital etc), dressed up in slightly different garb. Brett Silverstein's, *Fed Up! The Food Forces That Make You Fat, Sick and Poor*, published by the American Marxist publisher South End Press, is a classic example. (109) The book, in the author's words, "links increasing food prices and decreasing food quality, hunger throughout the world, and obesity in the US; racism, sexism, poverty and poor nutrition".

In Britain, Professor Richard Lacey's books push the same anti-capitalist credo. His *Unfit For Human Consumption: Food in Crisis – The Consequences of Putting Profit Before Safety*, is an attack on "the morality of the last decade when the primacy of the profit motive has eroded integrity, safety and compassion". (110)

Political vegetarianism is also particularly vigorous in targeting those "impressionable young minds" with its propaganda, frequently of a degree of illogicality and sick-making sentimentality that even largely uncritical journalists have commented that it is "carefully calculated to harness sentimentality, self-doubt, guilt and clubbishness. Logic is never allowed to get in the way of sentiment." (111)

Political vegetarianism has gone to the most absurd extremes to integrate every form of puerile sanctified "PC" posturing into their cause. My own favourite example is Carol J. Adams' *The Sexual Politics of Meat: A Feminist Vegetarian Critical Theory*. (112) At first sight you think that you have stumbled upon an extended parody of the sort might find in *Private Eye* or *Viz*'s "Modern Parents" strip. But Adam's actually means it. That such a work could be published by an academic publisher house – Polity Press of Cambridge – only shows the utter degradation of contemporary scholarship, and the strength of both "political correctness" and political vegetarianism.

Adams' concern is to show, in her own words, the links between "animal oppression with all other forms of oppression". She is particularly keen to establish a historical and analytical demonology of virtue versus vice: socialism, feminism, lesbianism, racial equality and vegetarianism on one side, versus capitalist exploitation, rape, heterosexual "patriarchal" oppression, racism and meat-eating on the other. Her claims – they can hardly be called arguments – are breathtaking:

"The presence of meat proclaims the disempowering of women"

"Eat rice. Have faith in women. Our daily diet reflects and reinforces our cosmology, our politics. It is as though we could say 'eating rice is faith in women'" ("Epilogue: Destabilising Patriarchal Consumption"

"If you are a piece of meat you are subject to a knife ... Rape too is the implementation of violence in which the penis is the implement of violence."

"The hearty meat eater ... is not only a symbol of male power, it's an index of racism."

"Meat eating is to animals what white racism is to people of colour, anti-semitism is to Jewish people, homophobia is to gay men and lesbians." (113)

Other academic apologias for political vegetarianism, marginally less potty than that of Adams's, includes Colin *Spencer's The Heretics Feast: A History of Vegetarianism* (114) . Spencer does his best to convince us that vegetarians constitute the best minds and finest spirits throughout the ages – but does not dissuade us from the famous observation of George Orwell, that they are in reality generally the nutters, cranks, wierdos and monomaniacs.

More in the spirit of the wonderful Ms. Adams is *Cooking, Eating, Thinking: Transformative Philosophies of Food*, edited by Deane W. Curtin and Lisa M. Heldke. (115) In typical "post-modernist" style its contributors ransack recipe books, mystical tracts, poems, sermons, ecological pseudo-science, vegetarian pronouncements, and eastern religions to buttress the claim that vegetarianism is a superior way of life.

Such is the vigour of food fascism and political vegetarianism that at least one journalist has predicted that:

> "Within 50 years people who eat red meat or drink alcohol will be ostracised. At social gatherings they will be able to indulge in these unhealthy – nay, barbarous – habits only after seeking the express permission of their disdainful companions. The vegetarian, teetotal majority will have enacted stiff laws to regulate those dangerous substances and will be especially vigilant in protecting the young. Studies will have shown that most carnivores take up their bad habit in childhood, before they can appreciate the force of the arguments against meat.

You may dismiss this as a ridiculous fantasy. Yet who would have dreamt that US public sentiment could shift so decisively against cigarettes?" (116)

IV: THE WAR AGAINST ALCOHOL

Historically religious bigots, tyrants, coercive paternalists, bureaucrats, "progressive" social engineers alike have never seemed to forgive alcohol for the crime of being so universally enjoyable. And even the disastrous failure of alcohol prohibition in the USA has not satisfied their thirst for power. Unsurprisingly, then, the next principal target of the health fascists after food has undoubtedly been that of alcohol.

Again, a mere selection of press coverage gives one a taste of its predominant flavour:

"Alcohol 'Kills 500 a Week' "

"The estimate is one of the highest produced in Britain for deaths from alcohol-related causes. Dr. Peter Anderson, community medicine specialist with Oxfordshire Health Authority, calculates in the *British Medical Journal* that 28,000 such deaths occur annually in England and Wales." (*The Times*, 25th September 1988)

"Working-Hours Alcohol Ban Wins Support"

"Drinking alcohol during working hours should be banned, a survey of personnel managers said yesterday. More companies are likely to impose bans in line with the recommendations of more than eight out of 10 managers in the survey. Figures produced by the Alcohol Concern charity estimated up to 14 million working days are lost every year through excessive drinking ... at a cost of £800 million." (*The Daily Telegraph*, 19th November 1991)

"Drink 'Damaging Health of 1.4 Million'"

"An estimated 1.4 million drinkers are damaging their health by exceeding the harmful level of 50 units of alcohol a week for men and 35 units for women, according to a government report published yesterday." (*The Guardian*, 12th December 1991)

"Parents Sue Distillers over Birth Defects"

"America's distillers are anxiously watching the first of a series of legal actions in which they are being blamed for causing birth defects". (*The Daily Telegraph*, 26 April 1989, p. 5)

"Drink-Related Cases Filling Hospital Beds"

"One in five hospital beds is occupied by a drink-related case, a Government-organised conference in London on women and alcohol heard yesterday." (*The Daily Telegraph*, 3rd December 1991)

"Drinking Costs Firms £700m"

"Ten percent of male workers drink alcohol heavily and take sick leave as a result, according to government studies published yesterday." (*The Times*, 5th December 1991).

"Alcohol and Tobacco Laws Under Fire"

"The Government was accused yesterday of adopting 'loony libertarian' policies which were frustrating attempts to cut the death toll from alcohol and tobacco abuse. Dr. James Dunbar, the director of the Tayside Safe Driving Project, criticised the prevailing attitude that placed greater importance on protecting individual liberty than on instituting effective policies, such as the introduction of random breath testing ... He said that there were also loony libertarians in the Labour Party when it came to this issue. And Mr. Peter Taylor, a broadcaster and author, who has written a book on the politics of tobacco, said it was the same attitude that was preventing an advertising ban being introduced on cigarettes. 'The argument used is that such a ban on what is a legal product constitutes an attack on liberty, but until advertising is banned it is going to be difficult for health educators to get their message across', he said." (*The Scotsman*, 4th November 1988)

"Dying for a Drink?"

A "special 22-page report" consisting of several virulently anti-alcohol articles, which include the following passages:

"The trouble with alcohol is people exactly like you. Statistically, you are unlikely to be an alcoholic, a lager-lout or a drunken driver. Yet the overwhelming probability is that you belong to a group who cause more damage – to society and to themselves – than all the habitual drunkards who ever lived. YOU ARE A MODERATE DRINKER ..."

"Every time you accept an alcoholic drink, you say yes to a depressant drug that will destabilise your brain cells, distort your personality and take the edge off your sex life. How much of this can your body take?" (*The Sunday Times*, magazine section, 19th February 1989, pp. 21, 36-37)

"Cancer Risk in a Beer a Day"

"People who drink more than seven pints of beer a week are three times more at risk from cancer of the pancreas, according to a... report in the International Journal of Cancer." (*The Guardian*, 5th April 1989)

"Parents Blamed for Rising Alcohol Abuse among Young Pupils"

"Parents who give their children a glass of wine with their Sunday lunch could be leading them into a life of alcoholism, a teachers' union leader said yesterday."

(*The Times*, 1st April 1989.

Unfortunately, this item does not appear to be intended as an April Fool's Day joke.)

"Children Tell of Thousands Topping Adult Drink Limit".

"Nearly 35,000 children a week drink more alcohol than the safe limit for adults, survey findings show ... as the Drinkwise campaign was launched ... 'It is estimated from this survey that 130,000 children under the age of 16 claim to be drinking alcohol regularly in pubs', the [Health Education Authority] says." (*The Guardian*, 12 June, 1990)

"What's Your Poison?"

"As a result of their consumption of alcohol 25,000-40,000 people die each year in England and Wales ... It is estimated that 30 per cent of child abuse, 78 per cent of assaults, 40 per cent of domestic violence, and 88 per cent of criminal damage is related to alcohol consumption (these are all probable underestimates) ... One way to reduce consumption is to cut advertising ... There is little doubt that the most effective way of reducing consumption is through raising prices via taxation." (*The Guardian*, 19th October 1988)

"Big Breweries 'Promoting Lager Violence'"

"Big brewers are both promoting and profiting from 'lager lout' violence, according to the real ale campaigner Ms Andrea Gillies. By putting forward a macho image for lager the brewers encouraged drunken violence among young men, said Ms Gillies." (*The Guardian*, 25th October 1988)

"Anger Over Carlsberg's £18 Million Ad Campaign"

"Brewing giant Carlsberg was criticised yesterday for increasing its advertising budget by 70 per cent despite rising worries over the problem of 'lager louts'. Its announcement of a new £18 million campaign dismayed politicians, police and alcohol-abuse campaigners concerned by a rise in drink-related violence." (*The Daily Mail*, 4th November 1988)

"Young Soak Up TV Alcohol Commercials"

"More than 60 per cent of young people aged 10 to 17 could identify at least four out of nine alcoholic drinks when they were shown still pictures from television commercials, according to findings published in the British Journal of Addiction this week." (*The Guardian*, 14th December 1988)

"Charity Urges Ban on Syringe Cocktails".

"The health department has been asked to halt the sale of cocktails served in large plastic syringes that are said to encourage alcohol abuse among teenagers ... Alcohol Concern has complained to the makers and to the health dept. The charity, which was set up to combat alcohol abuse, says that the packaging is aimed at teenagers. Tony Humphries of Alcohol Concern said: 'The fact that they are packaged in syringes links them to the excitement of taking drugs and puts them into the realms of the quick fix. They are clearly designed to encourage out-of-control drinking, simply to get drunk, and the way they are presented is clearly designed to appeal to very young people'." (*The Times*, 26 March 1992)

"Home Office Adviser Links Youth Drinking With Aids"

"A dangerous link exists between youth drinking and the spread of Aids which must be broken, the chairwoman of the Home Office working group on young people and alcohol, Lady Masham, claimed yesterday ... 'The young socialise in pubs. There's alcohol, then there's sex, then there's Aids. Alcohol relaxes them, makes them go over the top and lose control. Anything that can help prevent this should be done.'" (*The Guardian*, 26th October 1988)

"The Seduction of the Teeny Tipplers"

"Some poison is legal. And it's legal to advertise. It's even legal to make it attractive by surrounding it with pop music, celebrities, humour and radical chic. A recent study from Strathclyde University showed that, despite alcohol industry denials, glamorous commercials encourage under-age drinking"

"Too Much Too Young Cut Price Alcohol is a Danger to the Inexperienced"
(*The Times*, 11 September 1992, p. 5)

"Restrictions on Outlets 'Can Reduce Drink Flashpoints'".

"Magistrates can help cut violence and vandalism by restricting licensed premises in some areas, Mr David Waddington, Home Secretary, said yesterday. In urging licensing benches to show restraint, he said recent evidence showed that the presence of too many public houses, restaurants or off-licences in a locality could act as an 'alcohol flashpoint'." (*The Times*, 20th February 1990)

"Drugs Conference to Debate Desirability of Ban"

"Doctors and academics at an international alcohol conference are to debate calls for a world- wide ban on alcohol. The 36th Congress on Alcohol and drug Dependency, which opened yesterday in Glasgow will discuss whether a total ban on alcohol is a realistic or medically worthwhile goal." (*The Independent*, 18th August 1992)

The consumption of drinks which have been brewed, fermented or distilled to produce ethanol has been with humanity for thousands of years, probably since before the appearance of civilisation itself. Certainly Egyptian physicians were prescribing it before the pyramids were built, and its medicinal properties are still recognised today. Dr. Thomas Stuttaford, visiting physician to the BUPA Medical Centre, a partner in a London medical practice, and Times medical correspondent, explains:

> "For over 90 per cent of British adults, alcohol is an accepted part of their life ... Alcohol taken wisely, induces a feeling of relaxation which evaporates shyness and encourages friendship. Giving or accepting a drink strengthens bonds within friendships or families; it plays a part in all the important rituals which mark the passage of a lifetime, from the initial Christening to the final funeral; with it hopes for the future are toasted, successes celebrated and sorrows eased ... Taking alcohol in moderate amounts, so called sensible drinking, is beneficial. It reduces the chance of cardiovascular disease, particularly coronary thrombosis. It relieves stress in a wide range of age groups. It improves the quality of life in the elderly. It is a source of nutrition; it provides calories without fat, several trace elements, some of which, such as copper, although essential for the smooth running of the heart are in short supply in a diet which relies heavily upon convenience foods ... [T]he line of the graph which relates death from cardiovascular disease is U-shaped. The tee-totallers and the very light drinkers have a relatively high incidence of heart disease, the moderate social drinkers form the base of the U and do well, the heavy drinkers, for a variety of reasons do badly and form the other arm of the U." (117)

At least 19 studies around the world have shown that regular moderate alcohol consumption appears to greatly reduce the risk of heart disease, and wine drunk with meals seems particularly beneficial. For example, 1422 civil servants in London were followed up for 10 years: the mortality rate was lower in men reporting moderate alcohol intake than in either the non-drinkers or heavy drinkers, and heart disease was greatest in the non-drinkers. Statistics show a negative correlation between the mortality for cirrhosis (a statistic relied upon by the health activists to quantify intake in a community) and heart disease. An editorial in the American medical journal *Epidemiology* stated that there was now "compelling evidence" that "small to moderate amounts of alcohol are good for your health". (118)

Moderate amounts of alcohol help to prevent platelets (small blood cells) from sticking to fatty deposits on the artery wall, and thus 'sluice' the arteries. Red wine, in particular, increases the amount of high-density lipoproteins, which help to remove harmful cholesterol from the blood, in the bloodstream.

In addition, alcoholic drinks have great nutritional value. Beer and wine not only contain minerals and trace elements such as zinc, copper, manganese and potassium, but also many vitamins of the B group. Some wines and beer contain potassium salts, and were often recommended, before suitable potassium supplements were available, for the treatment of patients with renal and heart failure who were taking diuretics. Alcoholic drinks contain no fats and only traces of fatty acids, and thus have a role in cutting fat intake.

Moreover, as Dr. Stuttaford points out, "moderate amounts alcohol reduces anxiety, calms the emotions and thereby diminishes stress ... Scientific experiments have been used to show that alcohol diminishes tension, self-consciousness and depression, and increases conviviality." (119)

It is, however, difficult to be give a precise definition of "moderate drinking", because individuals, even of the same size and sex, differ considerably in their ability to metabolise alcohol, and in their reaction to it. When doctors discuss "safe levels", they tend to err on the side of caution, and set the level at a point where they are certain that nobody, however frail, small or inexperienced at drinking, is likely to suffer. They measure the "safe level" in terms of "units of alcohol", a unit of alcohol being regarded as a glass of wine, half a pint of beer or a pub measure of spirits. Yet wine and beer vary considerably in strength, and the measure of spirits differs in pubs, clubs and even by district.

The concept of "safe levels" of "units of alcohol" is therefore virtually meaningless when applied to millions of different individuals. But this does not stop the taxpayer-funded health activists from setting the "safe levels" of alcohol consumption lower and lower every year. For example, in 1989, in Britain it was announced that "low drinking" was up to three units a day in men and two in women; "moderate drinking" was five units in men and three in women; and "heavy drinking" was anything above this. Yet, as Dr. Stuttaford pointed out in 1989, "The biggest screening centre in London was until very recently still teaching that most men would be unlikely to suffer serious consequences of alcohol-induced disease at under 10 units a day, but to be safe it was wise to restrict the intake to six. It is unlikely that medical knowledge has substantially increased in the past year or two, thereby rendering this statement fallacious, more likely that the approach to the problem has altered in response to sociological pressures." (120)

So moderate drinking is not a health problem. On the contrary, it has many beneficial health effects. It is only excessive drinking that can in some cases lead to or aggravate health problems, but it is important to recognise that heavy alcohol consumption affects different individuals in remarkably different ways. For instance, liver disease is popularly considered to be caused by excessive alcohol consumption, but fatty infiltration of the liver can be due to a variety of causes, not just alcohol. Where it is caused by alcohol consumption, the liver usually returns to normal after the patient gives up alcohol. Cirrhosis is another disease which often occurs after years of heavy drinking, but alcohol over-indulgence is not the only cause: alcohol over-indulgence only causes cirrhosis in, at most, a third of cases. Indeed, the great majority of heavy drinkers fail to develop cirrhosis.

Many health activists claim that as many as a quarter of hospital admissions in Britain are due to alcohol consumption. For example, psychiatrists M.P Farrell and A.S. David argued in the *British Medical Journal* that, "alcohol has been estimated to be the cause directly or indirectly of about 27 per cent of acute medical admissions" (121). They thus argue that pressures on the National Health Service could be reduced by such measures as increased taxation and regulation on alcoholic drinks, in order to reduce consumption. Yet the facts cited above expose these claims as fallacious. If "moderate drinking" cannot be defined unambiguously, then neither can "alcohol misuse".

Many of the assumptions about what the effects of alcohol intake on the individual "should" be like have more to do with stereotypes and expectations than reality. A. M. Cooper, director of research at Human Relations Research Ltd, reports that:

> "[P]sychologists began using the double-blind method while observing behaviour in their labs. Some of the subjects who were told they were getting alcohol did get it and others didn't, while some of the subjects who were told they were not getting alcohol did, and others didn't. To a statistically significant degree, those who thought they had been drinking alcohol (but hadn't) showed more of the changes that are popularly associated with drinking than did those who had actually been drinking but thought they hadn't. This held true for sexual and verbal aggression, memory, facility with words, feelings of power, and even some measures of mechanical aptitude. The obverse was also true: those who drank but thought they hadn't were less affected than those who hadn't drunk but thought they had. In short, expectation (or expectancy) played a significant role in determining how much, or even whether, people were affected by a given dose of ethanol, under strictly controlled conditions.

"With such quantified evidence replicated on various populations in many countries, it is strange that so much is still written about the effects of alcohol as if they were automatic, mechanical and strictly dose-related." (122)

Needless to say, the health activists ignore these findings and not only claim that alcohol consumption is far more dangerous than it actually is, but also demand ever-increasing legal restrictions on the availability of alcoholic drinks to all consumers, including moderate drinkers. For instance, in 1988 the International Agency for Research on Cancer (IARC), a body of the World Health Organisation, issued a report which concluded that there was a positive correlation between the consumption of alcoholic drinks and the development of cancer in humans. Although there was no conclusive experimental evidence that alcohol was carcinogenic, the authors stated that the epidemiological evidence was so strong that they could only conclude that alcoholic drinks were indeed carcinogenic. (They also concluded that low and moderate alcoholic drinking carried no carcinogenic risk.) Yet the report selectively interprets the evidence in order to come to its main conclusion. For example, the study cites several studies of Mormons and Seventh Day Adventists, who do not drink alcohol, smoke or take tea or coffee, which show that they do indeed have a lower incidence of carcinoma of the oropharynx and oesophagus than the populations among whom they live. Yet the same studies also show a higher incidence of carcinoma of the prostrate and the central nervous system than in the control population.

Professor Kurt Hellmann is honorary consultant and visiting professor in the radiotherapy and oncology department of Westminster Hospital; has been head of the cancer chemotherapy department of the Imperial Cancer Research Fund, chairman of the European Organisation for Research on Treatment of Cancer Metastasis Project Group, president of the oncology section of the Royal Society of Medicine and chairman of the British Association for Cancer Chemotherapy of Solid Tumours; has edited five books (mostly on cancer chemotherapy); and founded and edited the professional scientific journals Cancer Treatment Reviews and Clinical and Experimental Metastasis. Professor Hellman comments:

> "It would be difficult to accept ... that the abstinence from alcohol is responsible for the lower incidence of carcinoma of the oropharynx in this population without also accepting that it is responsible for the higher incidence of carcinoma of the prostrate and the central nervous system.

> "The real problem in assessing epidemiological evidence, however obtained, is that even positive correlation cannot prove causation; neither does negative correlation necessarily mean that the factors under investigation are not responsible ... All that one can conclude at the present time seems to be that the direct carcinogenicity of alcohol if it exists, is only manifest under most complex circumstances in which other environmental factors are needed to play a decisive role. Contrary therefore to the IARC expert opinion, there is in my judgment insufficient evidence to unqualifiedly label ethyl alcoholic beverages per se as direct carcinogens to humans." (123)

Needless to say, journalists, who, as always, are looking for a "sensation", ignore such considerations in their coverage of claims about the supposed dangers of alcohol consumption. The examples quoted at the beginning of this section amply demonstrate the degree of scientific objectivity which governs journalistic coverage of these issues.

In spite of the challenges to their claims about the supposedly harmful effects of alcohol consumption, the health activists continue to demand ever greater legal restrictions on the availability of alcoholic drinks to the public. In seeking to substantiate these demands, the health activists cite a monograph compiled by Kettil Bruun, et al, in 1978, which compared historical trends concerning death from liver cirrhosis in various countries and concluded that "changes in the overall consumption of alcoholic beverages have a bearing on the health of the people in any society. Alcohol control measures can be used to limit consumption: thus control of alcohol availability becomes a public health issue." (124)

Yet subsequent attempts to find out exactly what bearing such changes in consumption have had on health have discovered a remarkable lack of uniformity. For example, in the report of the International Study of Alcohol Control Experiences (ISACE) in seven western European nations, sponsored by the World Health Organisation, a United Nations body lavishly financed by Western taxpayers, Makela, et al, admitted that:

> "Between different cultures, we found considerable differences in the level of problems of any given kind that are attached to a given level of consumption. Even in a given cultural setting, the relationship between consumption and problems is by no means a simple one." (125)

In the same report they went on to concede that, when looking at diseases other than cirrhosis, "Relations of alcohol consumption level and patterns to casualties and social problems associated with drinking are far less clear and universal ... In cross-sectional comparison of societies, correlation of these problems with consumption level are frequently negligible or negative." (126)

Yet in spite of these conclusions by his own organisation's study, the director-general of WHO has asserted that "Any reduction in per capita consumption will be attended by a significant decrease in alcohol-related problems". (127) This is clearly nonsense, and it is hard to see how such a claim could be made in good faith.

And of course WHO, a regular source of disinformation and committed to a political philosophy resembling both Fascism and Communism (128), has come up with a long list of further restrictions on the availability of alcohol to the public which it urges on governments. It argues that "If WHO does not take this lead, then the world can look forward to further increases in alcohol consumption and to ever-mounting casualty rates from the awful battlefield of alcohol- related problems, until health for all by the year 2000 becomes a very hollow toast indeed." (129)

(This is a reference to WHO's extraordinary slogan, "Health for all by the year 2000". Does this mean that millions of chronically ill patients are going to be cured by this date as a result of the decrees of WHO?)

1: Policy Claims Analysed

The following list includes some of the restrictions urged by health-activist organisations such as WHO, followed by comments on what has actually happened when these restrictions have been put into practice:

(1) Increased taxes on all alcoholic drinks to make drinking more costly, and the restriction or removal of duty-free sales on ships, aeroplanes, at airports, military bases, and so on.

Some of the countries where alcohol is most heavily taxed (such as Britain, the Irish Republic, the US, Canada and especially the Scandinavian countries) appear to have relatively high rates of drinking problems, while some of the countries with relatively low taxes (including Italy, Spain and Portugal) have relatively few such problems. The evidence suggests that when alcohol is heavily taxed, moderate drinkers (for whom there are positive health benefits to drinking) cut back their consumption, while heavy drinkers simply reduce spending on such items as food or clothing for their children in order to find the extra money for alcohol.

(2) Stricter regulation of sales, with licensing limited to fewer places, shorter hours, and effectively isolated from groceries, petrol and other common commodities.

Restricting the number of outlets has little effect on overall sales in various jurisdictions, and shortening the hours of sale tends to change the time, but not the amount, people drink. Indeed, if the example of Scotland, where licensing laws were liberalised under the Licensing (Scotland) Act 1976, is anything to go by, then when public houses are allowed to remain open longer hours, drinking problems tend to drastically decrease. Before the 1976 Act, licensed premises were only allowed to be open between 11am and 2.30pm, and 5pm and 10pm, and were prohibited from opening on Sundays The Act permitted licensed premises to remain open considerably longer, seven days a week, and in Edinburgh and Glasgow it became possible to drink continuously between 6am and 4am, by moving from one licensed premises to another.

According to Dr. C. Clayson, architect of the Scottish reforms, before 1976 "in every index for studying the misuse of alcohol the Scots were worse than the English. Personal or family drink problems, breaches of the peace, drunkenness, and drunk driving were all two or three times as bad in Scotland. So were admissions to psychiatric hospitals for the treatment of alcohol related disorders, and so also were deaths from cirrhosis of the liver." (130)

In 1974, before the reforms, the average Scottish family spent 11% more on drink than the UK average; by 1983, the average Scottish family was spending 7% less than the UK average. In 1978, a survey by the social surveys division of the Office of Population Censuses and Surveys before and after the changes found that the Scottish public had reduced its rate of consumption slightly and showed "a significant reduction in the pattern of acceleration in drinking towards the end of the evening. Thus although the 'beat the clock' attitude to drinking has not disappeared it has at least diminished." (131)

A 1985 survey by the OPCS noted an increase in alcohol consumption among women and concluded that "it results from a change in Scotland to a more relaxed attitude towards drinking in general, and in particular towards women's drinking. It is perhaps because of this more relaxed approach to drinking that more women now drink in public houses, and that the extensions to licensing hours brought about by the 1976 Act tend to be seen as having led to more sensible drinking, rather than as offering a temptation for people to drink more." (132)

In addition, there has been virtually no change in the number of breaches of the peace before and after the changes. Convictions for drunk driving rose in Scotland by 1.2% compared with 36% in England and Wales, and for violence against the person by 16.7%, compared with 43.8% south of the border. Convictions for drunkenness alone fell by 13.6% in the five years following the change, compared with a rise of 13.1% in England and Wales, and the number has continued to fall substantially since then. Convictions for under-age drinking fell by 18.6% in the four years following reform, compared with a rise of over 23% in England and Wales: one aim of the Act was to create a climate in which children could accompany their parents. In 1986, the *British Medical Journal* found that in Scotland the risk relative to England and Wales of having to enter a psychiatric hospital due to alcohol abuse had dropped by nearly half since the reforms.

(3) Either the outlawing of alcohol advertising, or its prohibition from selected media (radio and television), and restrictions on the content of such advertising, for instance so as not to appeal to women, young people or ethnic minorities.

Advertising tends to follow, rather than lead, sales, with the aim of securing a brand's share of the limited market. Greatly increased advertising expenditures in the 1980s coincided with falling sales in most parts of western Europe and North America. Consumption of alcohol continually increased in Russia and eastern Europe during the period of communist rule, despite the complete absence of alcohol (or any other) advertising. In France, the advertising of whisky has been banned since 1957. In that year, whisky imports were 157,000 proof gallons; by 1979 they totaled 6,294,000 proof gallons. Researchers have found very little correlation between exposure to alcohol advertising and alcohol consumption. On behalf of the Advertising Association, M. J. Waterson reviewed a large body of research from all over the world, most of it from non-industry sources, and concluded that it "clearly suggests that advertising has little or no impact on mature alcohol markets, other than at the brand level." (133)

Low-quality fortified wines, such as Thunderbird, are not advertised, but are heavily consumed by the homeless and poor. After thoroughly examining evidence from around the world, R. G. Smart, of the Addiction Research Foundation of Toronto, found that:

"The evidence indicates that advertising bans do not reduce alcohol sales, total advertising expenditures have no reliable correlation with sales of alcoholic beverages, and that experimental studies typically show no effect of advertising on actual consumption." (134)

(4) Signs in retail outlets, labels on bottles and messages on advertisements to warn potential consumers of risks associated with excessive alcohol consumption.

Warning labels about health risks are compulsory in the US, Mexico and Hungary, and have had little apparent effect, no more than warning labels on tobacco products.

(5) Imposition of a minimum legal age for purchase of alcoholic drinks, or increasing that age (generally to 21).

No correlation has been shown between drinking problems and traffic fatalities among young people and the legal availability of alcohol to them. Indeed, psychologists R. Engs and D. J. Hanson have suggested that in some instances the imposition of age restrictions has been counter-productive, as young people have rebelled against them by drinking even more than they did before the restrictions were introduced.

(6) Publicising the names of those who refuse to submit to a police-administered test of blood- alcohol level (BAL), confiscation of driving licence or vehicle of individuals driving with a measurable BAL, indexing the price of alcoholic drinks to ensure they rise in tandem with other goods, decreasing the alcohol content of drinks, forbidding discounts on sales, rationing to individuals or households and complete prohibition.

Rationing was attempted in most Scandinavian countries earlier this century, and rapidly abandoned. In countries where absolute prohibition has been attempted (including Tsarist Russia, the US, India and Iceland), a great deal of illegal production has followed, leading to deaths and blindings from poisoning and widespread disregard for the law. In the US, many local jurisdictions still remain "dry", and alcohol-related traffic accidents, arrests and other problems are often more prevalent in these areas than in neighbouring areas where alcohol sales are permitted. In the Soviet Union a massive anti-alcohol campaign was launched in the mid-1980s, including the curtailment of sales outlet and hours of sale, the imposition of severe penalties for offences such as public drunkenness and absenteeism due to drinking and a great reduction in the production and distribution of alcohol in state-owned agriculture and industry. A widespread home-industry of illicit distillation quickly appeared, together with a severe shortage of sugar for other purposes, and virtually all these restrictions were lifted in 1988, together with a government admission that these controls had failed.

In spite of the failure of such restrictions, many researchers in the field of alcohol abuse continue to urge them, because of political pressures. M. J. van Iwaarden, for instance, found no evidence that restrictions on advertising for alcohol would be effective, but nevertheless recommended them: "Banning radio and television commercials is likely to be the most promising approach, not because of its effects on consumption and abuse, but from a socio-political viewpoint." (135)

Needless to say, the health activists demand ever-increasing governmental coercive controls, and ignore the fact that people are far more responsive to what sociologists call "informal controls" (a form of what Hayek would have termed "spontaneous order"), in which individuals learn moderate habits of drinking as they grow up in a given social context. For example, in many social groups, including Orthodox and Conservative Jews and Armenians throughout the world, and viticultural groups in southern European countries, virtually everyone, including young children, drinks in a customary manner, but there are few heavy drinkers or alcohol-related problems. In Britain, too, sensible parents initiate their children into sensible drinking by a moderate approach. Children are first introduced to alcohol in the family home through a small glass of wine at Christmas or small whisky at New Year, and as they become older the alcohol dose goes up and the occasions become more frequent. Then the drinking takes place in the homes of adult relatives and contemporaries under adult supervision, and thence into the public drinking domain, where drinking as a peer activity takes place. For most drinking adults, this socialisation process is a successful one. As Professor Dwight B. Heath, professor of anthropology at Brown University, puts it:

"The choice is not between control and the absence of control. The important choice is between formal controls imposed from without, which restrict individual liberties and often trigger reactive asocial or antisocial patterns of behaviour, and informal controls shared by other members of one's community and likely to be not only accepted but highly valued by most people." (136)

2: The Campaigning Groups

It is notable that the anti-alcohol group, "Action on Alcohol Abuse", was set up in September of October 1983 by Mike Daube, the former Secretary of Action on Smoking and Health, and with the same sort of backing from the Royal College of Physicians. Its demands are virtually identical: restrictions on points of sale, advertising bans, health warnings on alcohol, increased health "education", increased taxation and opposition to any liberalisation of licensing hours. Fortunately (if surprisingly), the extremism of its approach led the government to withdraw its funding. Its Director at that point played the usual pressure group game of musical chairs and moved to one of the heart disease campaigns. The war is continued, however, by Alcohol Concern, the Kings College Health Fund, the Health Education Authority – which has established an annual "National Drinkwise Day" – the Institute of Alcohol Studies (a misleadingly objective name for a vitriolic offshoot of the "temperance" movement), and, of course, the British Medical Association. The British Medical Association has called for total bans on alcohol advertising and increased taxation. (137) The "Advertising Research Unit" at Strathclyde University also adds its weight to the campaign by producing hostile and contentious claims regarding both tobacco and alcohol advertising.

V: THE WAR AGAINST BOXING

"The Noble Art of Brain Damage".

"A serious health warning should be attached to boxing as to cigarettes."
(*The Times*, 9 May, 1986)

It is an unfortunate fact that the organised medical profession, to which the state grants considerable monopoly powers, is by no means a voice of circumspection, restraint and reason when it comes to the question of health scares. The medical profession as a body – although, happily, not all individual doctors – tends to add its prestige to some of the most outrageous claims made by the health activists, rather than to the patient and complex researches that are the mark of the true scientist.

Nor is this a particularly recent development. The medical profession has never really been noted for its acuity in scientific judgment. It is, after all, notorious for its opposition to major medical discoveries, and to countless beneficial therapeutic innovations (especially those not resulting in enhanced financial opportunities for doctors), from anaesthesia to osteopathy. Even now, a large amount of medical practice actually consists of practices whose efficacy has never really been scientifically tested or validated. The concept of "evidence based medicine" (ie of trying to discover whether treatments are actually doing your patients any good) is seen as revolutionary and controversial (138)

Neither is it new for the medical profession to engage in scaremongering. In Britain, when bicycles first appeared, doctors complained about supposed health risks, including "cyclist's spine" (back pain from leaning over the handlebars), "cyclist's faces" (facial disfigurement from over-exertion) and "cyclist's sore throat" (from the inhalation of bacteria). In 1895 a Dr. Herman warned in the *British Medical Journal* of the danger to women: "The side-to-side movement of the pelvis produces unnecessary strain on the back and loins and also friction against the sensitive external genitals and may lead to bruising, excoriations and other effects on the sexual system which we need not particularise." (139) Three years later, an editorial in the *British Medical Journal* warned that cycling was bad for the heart: "There must be few of us who have not seen the ill effects of over-exertion on a bicycle. It can produce dilation of the heart which shows the great strain put on it and can be very difficult to cure." (140)

We are of course, supposed to believe that reactionary opposition to progress and hysterical scaremongering are merely things of the past. Would that they were. Moreover, the privileged position of the medical profession tends to imbue it with an impertinent arrogance and both a personal and political paternalism. Historically, the medical profession in both Britain and elsewhere has frequently given support to statist and coercive policies of both "left" and "right", from eugenics, Social Darwinism and National Socialism to Fabian and Marxist forms of "public health". (141)

More recently, the *British Medical Journal*, *The Lancet* and the British Medical Association have gone beyond mere criticism, and have become highly politicised organisations, devoting a considerable proportion of their activity to making demands for ever-greater legislative restrictions and prohibitions on voluntary activities. All three organisations continuously lobby for such measures as the prohibition of tobacco and alcohol advertising and sponsorship of sporting and arts events, ever greater taxation on alcoholic drinks and cigarettes, and the extension of the compulsory seat-belt law to cover rear seat passengers.

One example of the profession's interference in individual liberty has been its demands for the prohibition of the sport of professional boxing, in spite of the fact that both professional and amateur boxing are already heavily regulated and subject to medical supervision. (It is a legal requirement that two doctors are on duty at every boxing tournament). In 1959, an editorial on boxing in *The Lancet* claimed that "as doctors we have a clear moral duty to fight for its total abolition." (142) At its annual representatives meeting in 1982, the British Medical Association began a campaign for Parliament to introduce a total ban on professional boxing, claiming that 337 boxers had died worldwide since 1945 as a result of injuries sustained in the ring, and that others had suffered blindness and brain damage. In 1984 the British Medical Association went further, and demanded the prohibition of even amateur boxing. (If this proposal became law, Britain would be the only country in the world where all boxing was illegal: in Sweden and Norway, the only countries in the world where professional boxing has been outlawed, amateur boxing is still permitted under strict regulation.)

The ideological themes in the British Medical Association's campaign against boxing and amongst its supporters are all very clear.

There is anti-capitalism:

> "Big money ... tempted young men", Dr. John Dawson argued in the 1984 British Medical Association report (Colin Gibson, "Doctors Fight to Win Ban on Boxing", *The Daily Telegraph*, 9 March 1984).

> "Money is at the root of all the arguments against the banning of boxing – money not for the fighters but for the promoters. It is about time that the 'working class' were treated as human beings and protected against the exploiters who seek to make money from their hardship and in the case of boxing, their lives" (M. L. Cross, "Letters", *The Guardian*, 26 September 1991)

There is further demonisation of the desire to make money, one very characteristic of monopolistic state-privileged professions like medicine (which produce ample amounts of money for their members):

> "Boxing was a way of making money out of organised brain damage" ("Doctors Take off Gloves Against Boxing", *The Guardian*, 8 July 1982)

There is blatant coercive paternalism:

> Boxing is "brutal", and therefore "society as a whole" (ie the British Medical Association and its chums) has a right to ban it, Dr. Vivian Nathanson, Head of Policy at the British Medical Association argued

("Time to Ring the Last Bell", *The Daily Express*, 16 October 1995, p. 5)

There is the bizarre claim that free choice is nonexistent:

In the words of Dr. Nathanson, again: "Up to now the consensus with the sports defenders and promoters has always been that people have a choice whether to box or not, that they are not forced into the ring, that boxers know the risks involved. Yet what choice is there really?" (*ibid*)

There is a tendentious, quasi-pacifist, class-biased 'exquisite' distaste for the realities of human life:

Boxing, a Labour Briefing, writer declares, is a "symptom of an uncivilised and barbarous society". (143) It manifests "animal urges" (144). "Boxing is not a sport, it is a criminal activity", in the words of Professor Ernst Jokl of Kentucky (145). Its fans are allegedly "sadistic" and "voyeuristic" (146) And the overweight paternalist Labour MP Roy Hattersley labels boxing" the "ignoble art" with no place in a "civilised society".(147)

In reality there have been only 14 deaths from boxing in Britain since 1946, far fewer than in many other sports, and, indeed, far fewer than the number of deaths caused by medical negligence and incompetence. As Dr. Michael Dinerstein, British Boxing Board of Control medical officer, commented, "If the British Medical Association wishes to ban boxing because of injury then it must advocate the banning of the Isle of Man TT racing, the Le Mans motor race, and parachute jumping. It must then consider the possible risks of hernia from stretching over a billiard table." (148)

One's only fear regarding such a point is the suspicion that many of the advocates of boxing prohibition would not be averse to such measures!

Another point was made by Jim Watt, former world lightweight champion:

"Doctors who think they can ban boxing are knuckle-heads. If they ban the sport they will just drive it underground and then it would be unsupervised, with no proper medical facilities. It would be a return to the days of the bare-fisted fights and then somebody would really get hurt." (149)

The results of all forms of prohibitionism, whether of alcohol, prostitution or whatever, is of course, never actually to eliminate the prohibited substance or activity. All that occurs is the driving underground of the activity, the worsening of the conditions of trade for all involved (participants, producers and customers), the destruction of common law legal and commercial safeguards and quality controls, the generation of super profits for criminal suppliers, the corruption of the police, and the generation of other forms of social disruption by the destruction of normal, informal, forms of (in the jargon of sociology) "social control" (but better termed by Hayek as "spontaneous order"). It is gratuitously tedious to have to point this out. The lessons of all forms of prohibitionism, the creation of "victimless crimes", is so well documented and widely understood, that one can only question the alleged humanity and intelligence of those who, like the British Medical Association, continue to campaign for them. (150)

Deaths in professional boxing ring are extremely rare, averaging less than one a year. Serious injury are far more common in other sports. The Royal Society for the Prevention of Accidents lists rugby union football as the most likely to cause lasting damage as a proportion of those participating. Back and spine injuries, and injuries to head, neck and eye are particularly common. Skating, racing, skiing and gymnastics all produce appalling disabilities. "Of all the sports, boxing is the least likely to put you in a wheelchair for life". (151)

As with other examples of health fascism, the treatment of scientific research by the advocates of bans and coercion, is something less than scrupulous.

Thus, When Richard Butler, a clinical psychologist at High Royds Hospital, in Leeds, conducted a study of 86 amateur boxers for a 2 year study that found memory and speed of functioning significantly improved (and was greater than players of other sports which were also tested), his findings were treated with a notable lack of enthusiasm by the medical establishment. Peer reviewers for the *Journal of Neurology*, asked for his findings to be toned down. In Butler's words:

> "The experts insisted we didn't make too much of the positive effects. The British Medical Association has a policy on banning boxing. The reviewers almost forced us to add statements playing the thing down". (152)

When the risks of boxing are debunked, however, the banners shift to another argument. What is important, apparently, is not the actual chances or extent of injury, but the fact that the sole purpose of boxing is attacking and allegedly injuring one's opponent.

But the goal of boxing is not to produce permanent physical damage. A knock-out or knock-down, although entailing risks, is not per se intended to injure). But the distinction between boxing and other contact sports, as Simon Jenkins has argued, is fanciful. The goal of all such sports is to establish physical supremacy over one's rivals. And although all have rules which intend to prohibit deliberate injury, in reality the purposeful infliction of injuries upon opponents is common. In Jenkins's words "Rugby union is a violent game that has long avoided proper regulation by being run by middle-class amateurs. The theory is that decent chaps do not realy kick heads, gouge eyes or crush vertabrae by collapsing the scrum. If they do, they are not prosecuted but 'sent off'". (153)

Jenkins also correctly points out the blatant class bias in the British Medical Association's campaign against boxing:

> "Boxing is the favoured spectacle of the working classes, nowadays sponsored by sharp-suited Cockney entrepreneurs ... As a result, it is awash with publicised tragedy. An injured boxer is always headline news, as is a corrupt promoter ... Boxing is sport stripped raw. As such you will never persuade middle-class opinion of its worth. Gentlemen sportsmen can dive with danger and take their own risks. The plebs must be protected from themselves and their pleasures." (154)

And the fact of this class bias draws us back to the other point made above. The mentality of the middle class British Medical Association supporter, and that of health fascists generally, is a PC revolt against real life. It is another manifestation of the revolt against life, of "resentment" and the "anti- life" nexus outlined and excoriated by such philosophers as Nietzsche and Ayn Rand. What the more naturally healthy "plebs" respond to is the reality of conflict, the virtues of toughness and courage, of facing fear, hardship and pain; of mastering a martial art, and achieving physical fitness. Boxing is a reminder of the realities of life that health fascism, so closely related to CND pacifism, animal-rights, vegetarianism and the whole drippy, touchy-feely world of so-called "progressivism". (155) And that is why, fundamentally, they want to ban it.

Virtually the only writer who recognised this was Frank Johnson, in a *Spectator* editorial:

> "Two men face each other on equal terms, aware of the danger of being hurt, injured and humiliated; but after the fight they generally accord each other marks of respect and affection ...

> Those who see only the cauliflower ears, bloody noses, punch-drunkenness and occasional deaths of boxing miss its genuine nobility ...

> Those who want to remove the reality of danger from all sports, to make them more contests of skill and nothing more, are impelled by motives which moved the Purtitans in Macaulay's famous apothegm about bear-baiting. The denial of pleasure to others is itself a very great, and much underestimated, pleasure ...

> The mountaineer knows that he is smaller by far than the mountain; the footballer that one day he might break his leg. The canoeist knows the danger of the rapids; the rugby forward knows that a clash of heads is bad for the neck. But a calculus of the tangible harms resulting from the facing of unnecessary danger is not an infallible guide to what is morally permissible and what is not. Nor is it the stuff of which our heroes are made". (156)

VI: THE WAR AGAINST GAMBLING

Again, gambling has always been a target of moralists and paternalists throughout the ages, and the war continues still. Of late the principal scare has largely focused on the evils of video games in amusement arcades:

"Arcades Face Ban on Young".

"Children under 16 could be banned from amusement arcades under proposals before Parliament ... 'we should protect them from the evil of gambling' [said Tory MP Patrick Thompson]." (*The Daily Express*, 17 May 1990)

However, it has been the establishment of the British National Lottery in 1995 that has really brought the anti-gambling lobby back into the headlines:

"New Gambling Addicts are Hooked on Lottery".

According to the Joseph Rowntree Foundation, scratch cards have increased "addictive gambling". They call for a state-run "Gambling Research Unit", and accuse the BBC in their coverage of the National Lottery of "coming close" to "aiming" at under 16s. (*The Evening Standard*, 17 July 1995, p. 17)

"Lottery Adds to Dangers of Ill-Health, say Doctors." (*The Times*, 17 July 1995)

"Losers in the Lottery"

"Playing the National Lottery could be bad for your health", says a report published today. A public health expert believes the lure of the lottery is putting other important aspects of life at risk. Poor people may be using the money they would spend on things good for their health to buy lottery tickets instead, says Martin McKee, of the London School of Hygiene and Tropical Medicine. 'Anything that makes poor people in Britain even poorer, especially if they do not derive benefits in kind, becomes an important public health issue', he writes in the *British Medical Journal*". (*The Daily Express*, 25 August, 1995, p. 19)

The inevitable pressure group, named, almost equally inevitably "The UK Forum on Young People and Gambling" pops up. Its Chairman, a lecturer in Psychology at the University of Plymouth, with all the usual arrogance of such paternalists who believe that only their view of what is "normal and socially acceptable", declares that:

> "By means of advertising and television coverage children are being introduced to the principles of gambling and will grow up to believe it is normal and socially acceptable." (157)

He similarly cites the Lottery's alleged role in "widen[ing] inequalities" and thus calls for "strict regulation", and, of course, "more research into the lottery's impact on family spending" (158) – i.e., more money extracted by force from the taxpayer to be given to him and his cronies to push their political agenda. Does one really have to belabour the point that in a free society it should be no concern of the state how free people spend their family income, or how "unequal" society is as a result of the choices, tastes and life decisions of individuals. That "social equality" might not even be perceived by everyone some as a desirable social virtue is similarly beyond his mental horizon.

And of course, there is our old friend the "protection of children":

> Rachel Sylvester, "Underage Gamblers Caught in the Act". (*The Sunday Telegraph*, 29 October 1995, p. 15)

> "Children at Risk ... Lottery 'breeding generation of gamblers".

> "Children as young as 13 are able to place bets illegally because bookmakers fail to ask them to produce proof of their age. A new study has shown that staff at the leading high street betting shops keen to win back business from the National Lottery, appear to be happy to turn a blind eye on underage betting ...

Dr. Mark Griffiths, senior lecturer in psychology at Nottingham Trent University, and author of *Adolescent Gambling*, said more children are becoming addicted to betting: six per cent of adolescents are gambling addicts, compared with only one percent of the adult population ... He said the National Lottery has encouraged children to bet: "Children are being socially conditioned to think that gambling is acceptable, that it is good and that they can take part in it". (159)

Griffiths also sent in a 15 year old agent provacateur into a number of gambling shops, and another anti-gambling pressure group, the National Council on Gambling, voiced their outrage at the appalling horrors of such an occurrence.

VI: "A PLAGUE OF HOBGOBLINS": THE DANGERS OF EVERYTHING

1: Everything?

At times, it seems as if the whole world is full of threats and dangers. Let us again survey some further examples from the press:

"Pet Birds Blamed for Lung Cancer"

"People who keep pet birds are more likely to develop lung cancer, doctors in Holland have found ... [P]eople who have kept birds at one time or another are seven times more likely to get lung cancer than people who have never kept birds ... [I]t may be that continuous bird keeping is as likely to cause lung cancer as continuous smoking." (*The Independent*, 18th November 1988)

"Doctors Call for Stricter Control Over Dogs as Public Health Risk Rises".

"Mans best friend can be one of his worst enemies when it comes to ill-health and accidents and much tougher controls are needed for dogs, according to doctors at Manchester University. The United Kingdom's six million dogs are responsible for more than 60,000 infections a year, 21,000 dog bites that need hospital treatment and road accidents that cost £40 million, Dr. David Baxter and Professor Ian Leck of the university's department of community medicine estimate". (*The Financial Times*, 4 September, 1984)

"Oftel to Close all Chatlines Next Month".

"Telephone chatlines, which have resulted in huge bills for addicted callers, are to be silenced next month". (*The Times*, 3 March 1992)

"Food Mixers & Vacuum Cleaners Linked to Cancer".

"Common household appliances such as food mixers and hair dryers send out enough electromagnetic radiation to induce cancer, coronary heart disease, and Parkinson's and Alzheimer's, according to a report leaked yesterday.

The report, for the National Council on Radiation Protection, radiation advisers to the American government, recommends a safety limit to exposure ... The report also backs up suspicions that schools and homes underneath high-voltage electricity pylons are at danger ..." (*The Daily Telegraph*, 5 October, 1995, p. 5)

"Hidden Hazards to Health in Every Home." (*Western Daily Press*, 5 October 1995)

"Talcum Alert After Eight Babies Die".

"Eight babies have died through inhaling talcum powder during nappy changes, doctors said yesterday." (*The Daily Telegraph*, 18 May 1991)

"Health Warning for Jumpers"

The Health and Safety Executive described bungee jumping as "inherently very dangerous", and attempted to restrict is spread in UK, citing the possibility of invoking the Heath & Safety Act at Work Act, 1974. (*The Daily Telegraph*, 18 October 1990)

"The Tragedy of Slipping on Soap Cannot Continue".

American safety activists have demanded safety ropes in all local shower baths. (*The Carolina Critic*, 5(4), October 15, 1991. p. 3)

"NatWest Tempts Teenagers into Debt with 'No Questions Asked' Cashcard." (*The Sunday Times*, 27 September, 1992, p. 5)

"Cancer Risk in 100,000 Households"

"About 100,000 homes in England – one in 200 – contain levels of radioactive radon gas which the Government regards as dangerous, according to a report yesterday. Radon, produced by uranium in the ground, causes lung cancer and may be responsible for 2,000 deaths a year." (*The Guardian*, 14th May 1992)

"Cancer-Causing Gas 'Widespread'". (*The Independent*, 26 October

1989)

"Thousands at Risk of Lung Cancer from Natural Radiation." (*The Glasgow Herald*, 16 March, 1989)

"2,500 Die from Rays in Their Homes". (*Today*, 26 October, 1989)

"Cancer Link to Vasectomy Detected."

"Men who have vasectomies may run four times the risk of developing cancer of the testicles, claims new research ... by doctors at Bangor General Hospital in West Lothian." (*The Guardian*, 9th February 1990)

"High Heat, Long Cooking a Cancer Risk, Study Shows".

"Frying or barbecuing meat, chicken or fish produces potentially cancer-causing substances [according to the] US National Cancer Institute." (*The Irish Times*, 27 March, 1991)

"Halogen Light 'Poses Cancer Risk'."

"Quartz halogen lamps, increasingly being installed at home and at work, may put people at risk of skin cancer, researchers claim." (*The Times*, 10th April 1990)

"Killer Plants for Sale at Garden Centres, Call for Warning Labels"

The National Poisons Unit called for all plants with poisonous leaves or berries to carry a skull and crossbones label. 13 "potentially deadly varieties" are on sale in the Swansea area, such as Columbine (its seeds contain acid, causing violent sickness); Holly Berries ("it takes only two to kill a child"); Oleander ("its poison, oleandrein, can kill in 24 hours"); tobacco (!) ("its leaves contain alkaloids which can cause weakened heartbeat, coma and death"); and Rhubarb (its "leaves cause extreme nausea"). TV gardener Geoffrey Smith says, "If it stops just one child being killed or hurt, it will have been justified."(!) (*The Sunday Express*, May 31, 1992, p. 6)

"Golf Concern"

Tricia Barnett, co-ordinator of "Golf Concern", stated on "World No Golf Day": "Golf courses, particularly in developing countries, frequently force people out of their homes and off the land, pollute the environment, and use up valuable national resources". (*The New Statesman*, 30 April, 1993, p. 7)

"Danger in the Potting Shed".

According to the Department of Trade and Industry's Consumer Safety Unit figures there are 200,000 accidents in gardens ever year. "Hidden danger lurks in the potting shed, with 2,000 gardeners injured by flower pots every year ... Feet are impaled by forks, eyes are injured by flying twigs from hedge trimmers and 10 people are electrocuted by their lawnmowers ... Flower pots lead to bruised feet, broken toes and crushed fingers, while spades and secateurs are responsible for 5,000 accidents a year". (*The Daily Telegraph*, 21 July, 1994)

Lord Falkland, Liberal Democrat, asked if government "would discourage spitting" because of the possible dangers of spreading tuberculosis, especially "new killer mutant strains" (Anthony Looch, "Question Time", *The Daily Telegraph*, 24 January, 1992)

"Sparks Fly Over Jeans Ad's 'Risk' to Macho Men".

"James Tye, director general of the British Safety Council, said the latest [Levi 501] ad was 'totally mindless and highly dangerous', and is writing to the Independent Broadcasting Authority demanding that it be banned. The story line is a role-reversed Cinderella, as a young woman with a pair of jeans goes in search of the man with narrow enough hips.

She finds her perfect fit in a workshop, a young mechanic already conveniently half out of his boiler suit.

Instead of a fairy tale Mr. Tye saw a death trap in which the Prince Charming character is seen to 'have total disregard for Health and Safety laws ... the semi-naked mechanic standing in a shower of sparks'. It would incite dangerous copy-cat exploits among apprentices." (*The Guardian*, 28 August, 1992)

"Hearing 'Can Be Ruined' by Night in Disco".

"Teachers and parents who warn about the horrors of drugs and disease seem to be unaware of the cruel dangers of excessive noise", according to the British Tinittus Association. Medical Research Council's Institute of Hearing Research, Dr. Ross Coles, also favoured noise controls. (*The Daily Telegraph*, 25 July 1994)

"Kissing Gets a Health Warning".

"A warning against heavy sensual kissing is being issued by the World Health Organisation for World Aids Day.

The warning, covering so-called French kissing, is the first time that the UN body has been so explicit over the risks of this kind of contact. Last year it would only go so far as declaring that 'kissing on the cheek' was safe". (*The Times*, 28 November 1991)

"School Loses Its Marbles."

The Headmistress of Hillside County First School has banned marbles in the playground "because she believes they are too dangerous". There are "fears that glass marbles could shed tiny shards and could cut or blind a child. No such accidents have occurred at the school but teachers have been concerned for some time. 'We decided that, before it became too dangerous, maybe it was time to call it a day'". (*The Times*, 18 November 1993, p. 3)

Dressed to Kill: The Link Between Breast Cancer and Bras (Book title, by Sidney Ross Singer & Soma Grismaijer, advertised in *The Tao of Books Catalogue*, p. 7)

"Addicted to an Idea of Love".

"Experts are beginning to see a worrying number of people addicted to personal advertisements. In fact, British Telecom contacted the Addiction Advisory Agency in London recently for advice on the phone contact advertisements that are becoming very popular ...This addiction may seem harmless, but it isn't. Besides the dangers from unwanted pregnancies, sexually transmitted diseases and potential violence, the cycle of building expectations up and having them knocked back again can lead to severe stress and depressive illnesses, especially if the person started using the adverts because they were shy or insecure." (*The Guardian*, Society supplement, 26 July 1995, pp. 2, 3)

War Toys:

> "According to two studies conducted by Dr. Thomas Radecki, children who play war games with 'superhero' dolls are twice as likely to get into fights and anti-social behaviour as children who play with non-violent figures such as the initial Cabbage Patch Dolls or Fraggle Rock toys". (*The Daily Telegraph*, 4 March 1986, p. 17)

And sometimes truth can be stranger – and sillier – than fiction. Both Digby Anderson and the ever astute adult comic *Viz*, have both written satires of the health and safety fanatics with spoof warnings about the dangers of Christmas. But neither was as funny as the real story run by *The Daily Star*:

> "It's Ho-Ho-Woe Time, Beware the 12 Dangers of Christmas."

> "Christmas crackers and frozen turkeys can be lethal weapons, a doctor warned festive merry- makers yesterday ... 'Every year you think you've seen it all, then something more ridiculous happens', said Dr. Susan Barnes, who runs the accident and emergency department at Dewsbury District Hospital in West Yorkshire ...

> Frozen turkeys cause us a lot of problems. People drop them and suffer broken bones in their feet. Others do their backs in lifting them out of the oven ... food poisoning cases because the turkeys haven't been thawed out or cooked properly ...Exploding Christmas crackers can also cause problems. People get eye injuries as the toys inside the cracker are thrown across the room ... electric shocks from dodgy lights on their trees ... Youngsters choking on toys after being left on their own ... Suffering burns when the decorations catch fire ... Girls cutting their feet on broken glass by dancing barefoot in clubs ... Children ... falling off [new bikes] on their first ride ... Dog bite injuries ... as pets get excited ... Teenage girls end up in hospital over Christmas with hypothermia after going out in freezing weather in skimpy party dresses". (*The Daily Star*, 6 December 1991, p. 8)

The temptation is to deal with this sort of thing merely in terms of humour, and to respond by ridicule. The journalist Craig Brown did so on one notable occasion. Writing in *The Evening Standard* he declared:

"Surely the most irritating of all programmes on television or radio is 'You and Yours' on Radio 4. It is the consumer programme gone mad, with four or five fresh moans every day, usually about domestic appliances, all of them ending with the traditional bellow: 'It's high time the Government did something about it'.

A day in the life of the average 'You and Yours' contributor must be grim indeed. Waking up in the morning, he discovers his blanket has slipped off his bed. He immediately writes a letter of complaint to the blanket manufacturers. Then he can't find any socks that match, so he sets about suing the sock manufacturers. At breakfast, his corn flakes run out, so he writes to You and Yours calling for legislation to force cereal manufacturers to fit battery-operated alarm systems an inch from the bottom of their packets.

Until last week, I thought 'You and Yours' had already covered every conceivable entry in the Wonderful World of Whines, and was simply repeating itself. But then I heard a special report claiming, in gravely tones, that the increasing popularity of helium balloons among children is proving a major environmental hazard, 'littering the countryside and posing a danger to wildlife'.

I have lived in the country all my life, and I can honestly say I have never once spotted the remains of a helium balloon, either as litter or in the mouth of a choking bunny-rabbit. As major hazards go, helium balloons are roughly on a par with candy-floss.

Whoops! Even now, I can see a bright young 'You and Yours' reservation sifting through the mail bags in search for a man who has been permanently blinded by a stick in his eye after a misplaced lunge at candy-floss, or a woman who bought candy-floss believing it to be a lovely pink wig for that extra special day, only to find it melting under the heat of the lights.

Deary me. 'You and Yours' is littering the country with complaints, posing a major hazard to the sanity of the nation. Frankly, it's high time the Government did something about it." (160)

2: Fragrance Fascism

Many of these alarms are self-evidently silly. Many suffer from the faults already indicated in our more detailed criticisms: Extrapolations on the basis of dubious methodological assumptions; lack of real evidence or proper testing; biased sampling; unrepresentative findings and so on. Some deserve more detailed comments however.

My own favourite from amongst the really silly scares is that of "fragrance fascism". As silly as this phenomenon is it has nevertheless already had a positive impact on policy in America. And where America leads, the rest of the world is sure to follow.

Fragrance fascism is the attack on "passive perfume" in the same manner, and with the same lack of real evidence, as that on "passive smoking".

"Perfume is going to be the tobacco smoke of tomorrow", a spokesman for the "Human Ecology Action League" has declared. "Second hand fragrance" is even labeled by the League as "scent rape" and the "Environmental Health Network", has broadened the issue to one of protecting the "chemically sensitive" from all forms of alleged harmful chemical substances in our everyday environment. Another spokesman, one Julia Kendall, of the "Chemical Injury Litigation Project", has also stated that:

> "No one should be wearing perfume to theatres. Why should we have brain damage because people are wearing toxic chemicals? ... Basically, we want to destroy the fragrance industry". (161)

The Asthma and Allergy Foundation of America has also called for a law against scented sample strips in glossy magazines, and bans its staff from wearing perfumes in office.

The University of Minnesota has adopted a "scent-free policy" to protect those with "multiple chemical sensitivities", and even the private sector has been infected with this hysteria. Jimmy's Place restaurant in Chicago, for example, banned perfume in 1991.

Mary Lamielle, President of National Centre for Environmental Health Strategies, has singled out "the power perfumes of the 1980s, such as Giorgio, that used highly allergenic chemicals" and cited favourably attempts by a number of local governments to establish "fragrance free zones" (162). In Marin County, California, environmentalists were trying to ban people wearing perfume from public meetings, libraries, hospitals and therapists. The California Air Resources Board also considered a proposal to totally ban sales of most perfumes. And the San Francisco mayor's office, has requested people at public meetings not to wear perfume, and instructed City Hall staff to refrain from using pungent cleaning substances if a visitor declares "environmental sensitivity". Pungent cleaning substances can even include new polish on shoes! (163)

Self-described "headache victim" Marjorie Crandall, in Torrence, California, has been campaigning to remove lavatory deodorisers from restaurant toilets. One west coast chain of cinemas actually responded to campaign by removing such air fresheners! (164)

And, as is to be expected in America, absurd legal cases have materialised. Bloomingdales' department store in New York paid $75,000 in an out of court settlement of an action by an asthmatic woman who claimed that she had landed in hospital for 11 weeks after being sprayed by perfume by a saleswoman. Using the Americans With Disabilities Act and subsidised with taxpayers money other alleged "multiple chemical sensitivity" victims are also filing suits.

3: Breast Implants

Another area where scare propaganda has an immediate policy impact is that of silicone breast implants. The American Food and Drug Agency (FDA) declared a moratorium on such breast implants in 1995.

Although a very few implants did leak, there is no evidence that small quantities of silicone are dangerous to the human body. Similarly, as with all operations, there are minor risks (such as scarring between the breast and the implant), but none that are life threatening or irreparable.

Nevertheless, the scaremongers made confident pronouncements, like that of Sidney Wolfe, Director of the Public Citizens Health Research Group: "Plain and simple, there is no public health need for these extremely unsafe devices to remain on the market. They are cosmetic devices for which far better alternatives exist"

And Dr. Scott Kale, rheumatologist at Rush Presbyterian St. Luke's and St. Josephs Hospital in Chicago, cites the threat connective issue diseases, and – typically – accused cosmetic surgeons of "vested interests".

The reality is that controlled tests in south east Scotland on 319 women with implants over last 10 years, found no evidence of any connective tissue disorders. A Mayo Clinic, Minnesota, study found that only five out of 750 women with implants developed connective tissue disorder over 8 years – a rate no higher than among the control group of 1,500 women with no implants (165)

Aside from the point that there is no evidence that breast implants are "extremely unsafe", consider the implications in Wolfe's view that an "unnecessary" device (in whose opinion?) that allegedly poses some risks should be banned as long as "better" alternatives exist. Should the contraceptive pill be banned because condoms or the rhythm method exist? Should tampons be banned because of the slight risk of toxic shock and because sanitary towels exist? And why should Mr. Wolfe be empowered to destroy women's free choices? (166)

So far, on this issue at least, sanity has prevailed in Britain. David Sharpe, consultant plastic surgeon at St. Luke's Hospital, Bradford has voiced the predominant medical view:

"[The FDA decision] doesn't seem to be based on any scientific evidence whatsoever ... The risk of breast cancer is infinitesimal. As for leakage, there have been 26 cases worldwide out of 3 million operations". (167)

4: The Video Games Scare

Another scare which has made an impact is that against computer video games:

"Video Games: Young People in the Firing Line".

"A recent television programme found that almost half the children at a school in Manchester showed signs of addiction to video games. Boys were more addicted than girls and they discovered than boys who regularly played video games were more aggressive than their class-mates." (*The Guardian*, Education Supplement, 13 April 1993, p. 8)

"Violent Games 'Hook' Young." (*The Guardian*, 15 February 1993)

"Screen Test for Young Video Addicts".

"A major study is to be carried out into the effects of video games on young people ... Expensive computer and television games have been criticised for turning young people into addicts and making them aggressive and antisocial". (*The Daily Telegraph*, 30 August 1993)

Thus, the Epilepsy Research Group at Queens Square has received funds from the Department of Trade and Industry to investigate the effects of video games in order to formulate "guidelines". It is notable that the Society's paper, in its coverage of this story complained about the fact that "There is a serious lack of funding for epilepsy research". (168). How useful a scare is in generating money! Thus, Lord Hastings, Chairman of the Epilepsy Research Foundation, predictably argues that parents should "err on the side of caution" regarding the video games as a possible cause of epileptic seizures". (169)

Legal craziness has, predictably, broken out in America. Already one

Michelle LaBruzzy, a 17 year old in Michigan, is suing Nintendo after developing an inflamed thumb from playing her home video game too much. She claims that her "Nintendinitis" prevents her writing and interferes with school work. (170)

The scare is very reminiscent of the moral panics over so-called "horror comics" in the 1950s and, more recently, the so-called "video nasties", and of equally little foundation. (171)

Jonathan Sigger and Dr. John Colwell of the School of Psychology at Middlesex University, found that boys of 13 and 14 who played computer games for long sessions had higher self- esteem and lower levels of aggression than those who did not.

Similarly, Dr. David Deutsch, Research Fellow at Wolfson College, Oxford, has argued that no real evidence against them, and that they are actually beneficial. In his view they "are par excellence a learning environment that is under one's own control, and that prevents them from being harmful". Indeed, he speculates that this is precisely the reason they are feared by those who identify "education" with coercion! (172)

5: The Electro-Magnetic Radiation Scare

More ominous in terms of its potential impact in Britain has been the electro-magnetic scare, as the following selection of press coverage shows:

"Power Line Cancer Fears Prompt Call for More Research"

"Growing concern that cancer may be linked to exposure to electromagnetic fields of power cables brought a call from leading scientists yesterday for more research. 'There are now so many studies which have shown this to be the case that it is difficult to avoid the conclusion that there is a significant health risk,' said Dr. Leslie Hawkins, of Surrey University." (*The Daily Telegraph*, 23rd March 1989.)

"Child Cancer Probe to Focus on Fears over Electricity"

"Cancer experts are planning the first nationwide investigation into links between electric blankets, home computers, pylons and childhood tumours." (*The Observer*, 24th June 1990.)

"Cancer 'Link With TV Transmitter' "

"An environmental medicine specialist called yesterday for an inquiry into a possible link between a 'cancer cluster' and a TV transmitter." (*The Guardian*, 30th March 1992.)

"Mobile Telephone Cancer Fears Are Real, Says Expert."

"Allegations that mobile phones' microwave emissions may be linked to cancer could be justifies, according to a leading scientist at Oxford University. Dr. Keith McLauchlian, a fellow of the Royal Society and an expert on the effect of microwaves on chemicals, said his research indicated that assurances put out by the mobile phone industry may be premature. The vested interests in believing [assurances of safety] is enormous". (*The Sunday Telegraph*, 7 February, 1993)

In America there has already been a legal case, one David Reynard, of Petersburg, Florida, having sued manufacturer and service provider for death of wife due to brain cancer, allegedly as a result of using her mobile phone.

One need spend little time in refuting the scare-mongering on this subject. As the late Professor Petr Beckman has declared, the fears of the alarmists are "sick fantasies ... buttressed with mantas in scientific jargon ... [that display a] contempt for causality and reliance on 'concurrency and contemporariness". (173)

Similarly, a two year study by Institution of Electrical Engineers has refuted fears, and the American Physical Society issued a statement Power Lines and Public Health declaring that there "is no consistent link between cancer and power lines" and "no plausible biophysical mechanisms" that could explain any alleged links. (174)

6: The Dental Mercury Scare

A BBC television Panorama documentary, "The Poison in Your Mouth", in July 1994 on the alleged threat to health of dental mercury amalgam in tooth fillings, constituted, as Dr. Simon Wesley declared in a rare but penetrating press critique, a classic example of the medical health scare. (175)

In spite of the fact that over 20 years a considerable literature on the subject has produced "little evidence ... to suggest any dangers", Panorama produced a programme that contained all the "essential elements of good medical scare stories".

The first is plausibility (in this case, mercury at certain levels is toxic), and the second is should be "near home". In Wesley's words:

> "[T]he threat must cause symptoms hard to verify, hard to disprove, but also extremely common. The programme began by listing the symptoms of amalgam poisoning as fatigue, poor concentration, insomnia and mood change. The fact that a major survey of the inhabitants of Gothenburg in Sweden had found no link between these symptoms and mercury fillings was not mentioned ...

> [F]rightening diseases of unknown aetiology should be part of the picture. An American researcher obligingly claimed that dental amalgams could cause Alzheimer's disease. The evidence was largely an unpublished neuro-psychological study which, we were told, will report subtle changes in concentration and attention in dental technicians. The researcher was certain 'that mercury caused these definite central nervous system deficits'. However, neuropsychological testing is extremely sensitive. Any abnormalities must be rigorously controlled and replicated, and can never prove cause and effect.

> [A]n absence of published research that does not support your case.

> For example, the commonest claim against dental amalgam is that leakage of mercury weakens the immune system leading to various disorders. Yet a Swedish study in the Archives of Environmental Heath this year found a weak link between the number of amalgam fillings and plasma mercury, but this did not correlate with any immune abnormalities. Instead they were linked to such unglamorous factors as

diet, hygiene and social class. The same group went on to show that there was no link between amalgam and a number of allergic or immunological diseases.

[T]he use of emotional language. This dental amalgam is a 'time bomb' and 'a growing threat', and new findings are always 'dramatic breakthroughs'. When evidence is doubtful there is a tendency to raise the stakes. Who could resist the pleas to 'think what this might do to the brains of young children'. Who would not share the concern that mercury could be transmitted to the unborn child – although no mention was made of a survey of 20,000 dental workers, which found no increase in spontaneous abortions or stillbirths?

A spokesperson for authority who can then be made to look complacent is [another] element. This role was played in [the] programme by the chief executive and the scientific adviser of the British Dental Association. They were confronted with new American research findings of unknown provenance and reliability. The credibility of the officials suffered merely because they had yet to consider this new work.

... when another authority figure, on this occasion the Department of Heath, refuses to take part (presumably because they can spot a mugging in advance), you can call this ignoring the evidence'". (176)

VIII: THE CRITIQUE OF HEALTH SCARES AND STATE PATERNALISM

A number of critics of the anti-smoking movement, like Bernard Levin, Keith Waterhouse, and Iain Murray were laughed at when they first warned that movement was a prelude to similar campaigns on other substances or lifestyles. "The most pernicious thing about smokism", declared Keith Waterhouse in 1986, "is that it is not really about smoking at all. Cigarettes happen to be the product the smokists currently want stamped out. Tomorrow it could be – and will be – white bread, or beer, or junk food, or mashed potatoes. The object of the exercise is to impose the will of those who believe they know best on a supine population which is supposed not to know enough to come in out of the rain". (177)

This paper has attempted to show that this is precisely what has occurred. Let us now offer a more detailed critique of the rise of health scares and health fascism.

1: The Discourse of Fear: Recurrent Themes in Health Scare Propaganda

The reaction to health scare propaganda by many people is increasingly one of growing weariness and cynicism. Health scares are put down merely to the natural tendency of the media to indulge in attention-grabbing headlines. But this is far too simplistic an approach, and one that ignores the real genesis of such alarms. We must examine the real "social construction of knowledge" – or, rather, of falsehood. Health scares do not appear out of thin air. They are the product of specific groups with specific interests.

Moreover, we must not underestimate the impact of the perpetual manufacture of scares and alarms. A comparison with the old Soviet Union is illuminating. Although large numbers of the enslaved citizenry of the old "evil empire" assumed that any specific propaganda claim made by their masters was a lie, the accumulation of propaganda, the recurrent themes, motifs, assumptions, and subtexts nevertheless still moulded the consciousness of its recipients. These are the "imperceptible" effects referred to Ellul, in our quotation from him at the start of this paper.

What is the subtext of health scare propaganda, and what is the purpose of its manufacturers?

The subtext is, of course, one of fear. The purpose of the propaganda is a general attitude of fear and apprehension regarding ones health, to see modern food and lifestyles as unhealthy, unhealthy as a result of the wicked capitalists concerned only with profit. Modern technology and scientific innovations, rather than blessings, are fraught with danger and risk. The world as a whole is seen as ever more full of risk. The deeper subtext is, of course, to disempower ordinary people. The expert, the medical authority, is imbued with (for some reason) an aura of both objectivity and benevolence. If the ordinary person is confused, cynical even, this too serves its role. The feeling that something is wrong, that risks do abound, even if one cannot be sure which are real and which false, still empowers the allegedly benevolent expert. "We are a nation at risk" is a frequent phrase used by the health fascists. (178) The lingering, nagging, persistent impression that "we are at risk" – this is the message of the endless alarmism. The endless harping on the threat to "children and young people" is a similarly crude appeal to the most atavistic levels of emotional functioning. It is designed to provoke not only fear, but hysteria, and to close the mind to rational thought. This is precisely the role of propaganda. Its purpose is not to convey knowledge, to stimulate thought, but to mobilise for action.

What we (and other writers) have referred to as "health fascism" and "food fascism", although having an ancestry going back to the 18th and 19th centuries (179) they have really emerged in the current "post-socialist" era. As the grand narrative of Marxism has self-destructed in theoretical confusion and chaos and in practical disaster for its victims (as did its shorter lived heretical variants of racial collectivism, National Socialism and Fascism), health fascism emerged as a significant force. Why should this be?

The answer can only be found in a class analysis. Marxism was never really an ideology of the "proletariat". It was always an ideology of its manufacturers, the intelligentsia. The masses have only ever been the metaphorical and literal canon-fodder of the intelligentsia, and the intelligentsia, in the form of the political and administrative ruling class, the only beneficiaries of Marxist rule. Many forms of class analysis tend only to see class interest in economic categories. They have been generally blind to the class interest of the intelligentsia, of what some have termed the "new class". (180)

As we have argued earlier, health fascism replaces many of the functional categories of Marxism with health-oriented ones. The result is, of course, still anti-capitalism, a view of the ordinary person that sees them as prone to "false consciousness" and unable to make truly free or wise decisions for themselves. Thus, the State must dictate to the masses for their own good, and suppress the wickedness of the profit-motivated "barons". Once again, the experts are to rule benevolently.

Health fascism overlaps especially with extreme environmentalism, which purveys much the same message of hysterical alarmism and falsification of evidence. The overlap becomes very clear in their common technophobia and opposition to industrial civilisation. (181)

In some respects health fascism is cruder than old-style Marxism. Marxism, at least, adopted the mantle of science and progress, and was frequently imbued with a technocratic vision and optimism. Health Fascism is more in keeping with the contemporary retreat from reason manifest in "post-modernism", hermeneutics, deconstructionism, social constructionism, environmentalism and the whole contemporary witches-brew of irrationalisms.

Marxism and other forms of older socialism, for all their errors, at least dealt primarily in a rational conceptual world, with issues of equality and justice, with economic analysis and political philosophy. But now "Nutrition is politics", as one French health fascist has declared. The propaganda of health fascism is, as one

French critic has pointed out, almost religious in nature, a playing with deeper realms of human insecurity and fear. It is more reminiscent of the earliest forms of what Marx called "Utopian Socialism", and of the myriad groups of millenarian religious cults in the middle ages. (182) The alleged dietary "plagues" of the West are portrayed as punishment for our sins, punishment for our very affluence and arrogance. As Pascal Bruckner has written:

> "Failures and distresses are collected because they serve as a clear warning – you have enjoyed yourselves too much ... Meat eaters are morally inferior ... Blessed are those who eat bulgur wheat and sorghum, for theirs is the kingdom of heaven! ... Meat is the root of all the evils of the West, and livestock suck the blood of the earth! But leeks, carrots, and celery will ensure the reconciliation of mankind!" (183)

A recent *Daily Telegraph* editorialist has similarly gone some of the way in understand what is happening:

> "(O)ur willingness to be alarmed by such warnings is, perhaps, connected to a deep and perverse human instinct.
>
> Since Prometheus was chastised for giving fire to mankind, and chained to a rock that a vulture might peck out his liver, mankind has irrationally expected to be punished for technological advance. In the Judeo-Christian tradition, it was Eve's plucking of the fruit from the Tree of Knowledge which led to the banishment of the human race from paradise. One may be prepared to believe that visual display units emit some sort of baleful ray. But hairdryers and food mixers have been with us since the 1950s. They are the symbols of capitalist triumph.
>
> It was the prospect of obtaining hairdryers and food mixers which drove the subjugated people of eastern Europe to throw down the Iron Curtain. We face a choice. Mankind can either listen to the technophobes, armed with probably tendentious scientific facts, and revert to an existence like that of the Amish people of America: living on withered and misshapen organically grown vegetables and commuting by horse-drawn buggy. Or else the human race can continue to exploit its enormous powers of invention in the cause of mixing cakes, and blow- drying its hair with almost certain impunity." (184)

A large literature on the sociology, anthropology and economics of risk has emerged in the last few decades, much of it very illuminating. To draw fully on it would lengthen this paper intolerably. Suffice it to say, what emerges most clearly is that the world, contrary to the assertions of the scaremongers of every sort, is becoming ever more safer. And the way to increased safety is not the fearful and obsessive fear of risk and the attempt to overcome it by state regulation, but by allowing full scope to freedom, free choice and innovation. Freer is safer – as well as more prosperous, more comfortable, and more just. (185)

2: The Religion of Health and the New Class

I am not the first, of course, to point out the vested class interests of the medical establishment and the health activists. Professor Peter Berger, of Boston University, for example, claims that health activism has become a new religion. As a result of the increasing affluence of recent decades, he argues, "Hypochondria and paranoia, which have always been inflictions of individuals, have now become very firmly institutionalised in most Western societies, and especially the United States, which is in the lead of this cultural change – indeed, of most cultural changes." (186)

This new religion has a large, and growing, professional priesthood of health activists, claiming to act in the public interest while actually pursuing an agenda hostile to market processes and individual liberty. Professor Berger describes this stratum as part of the "New Class", which, he says, "depends directly or indirectly upon government subsidisations and thus has a strong vested interest in the expansion of government services". (187)

3: The Complexity of Science

The argument of this essay does not depend upon every scare we have mentioned being false, or upon an assertion that no risks currently or in future reside in particular products or lifestyles. By chance alone the alarmists must have got something right. What is central to our case, however, is that the alarmists are abusing science for the sake of a political agenda.

A more general scientific critique of the alarmists can be delineated. The limitations of epidemiology will be discussed in the next section, but even more fundamental methodological criticisms can be made, especially in relation to the search for the causes of cancer. Even dedicated heath fascist Richard Peto, Director of Oxford University clinical trials unit, has admitted that some of contemporary cancer research is "just junk", and that exaggeration was occurring in order to win more funding. He criticised the "Scare of the Month" approach in USA and stated that "There's a hell of a lot of junk coming out under the guise of epidemiology" (188)

Other writers on the "cancer industry" question the premise that underlies virtually all the cancer scares: the dose response relationship. In other words, is the effect of a substance on health linear, ie, is there a harmful dose response relationship no matter how low a level of exposure to a substance, or is there a safe threshold, a cut-off point below which a substance has no harmful effects – or even possibly beneficial ones, the phenomenon of "hormesis". Thus, in the notorious Alar scam it subsequently emerged, in the words of Dr. Le Fanu, that:

> "[T]hat to get the dose equivalent of that fed to the rats which proved Alar's 'carcinogenity' [a human being] would have to drink 19,000 bottles of apple juice". (189)

There is now a growing American literature challenging the assumptions of orthodox cancer research, but unfortunately it is little known or distributed in Britain. (190)

Another fundamental challenge to the idea that perfect safety could ever be achieved is the existence of "biochemical individuality". As the leading proponent of this approach, Professor Roger Williams demonstrated, there are massive physiological differences between people. What might be beneficial for one person might be deadly for another. One person's nutritional requirements might be very different to another's. Thus, no drug could ever be totally safe. For someone it might have a deadly side-effect. Human variation and diversity were inherent and inevitable, and so were the subsequent risks that that fact entailed. (191)

4: The Corruption of Science

A disturbing aspect of the new health religion is that whole bodies of science are distorted in order to keep the flow of taxpayers' money coming in for research. Epidemiology, for example, was until about 1950 the study of the pattern of infectious diseases. However, because most infectious diseases have now been eradicated, epidemiologists now search for associations between "diseases of civilisation", meaning heart disease and cancer, and 'risk factors', which are either personal characteristics (such as age, sex, race, weight, height, diet, habits, customs and vices) or situational characteristics (such as geography, occupation, environment, air, water, sun, gross national product, stress and density of doctors). As the late Dr. Petr Skrabanek, then reader in community health at Trinity College, Dublin, explained, this enabled epidemiology to become a self-perpetuating process:

> "The association game has three possible outcomes: positive association, negative association, or no association. As any of these three outcomes are generally deemed to be 'interesting', 'controversial', or 'in need of further research', they all get published. 'No association' is an uncommon outcome, since in most studies at least 'a tendency towards' a positive or negative association can be shown. Considering how many cancers exist, and how many items of diet can be entered into the game, the number of possible combinations is staggering and opens new vistas for the generations of epidemiologists to come." (192)

For instance, epidemiologists have found that cabbage consumption is associated with both decreased and increased risk of cancer; and coffee consumption has been associated with both increased and decreased sexual drive and reproductive capacity. In a single edition of the *New England Journal of Medicine* in 1985, one article showed a significant negative association between oestrogen-replacement therapy and coronary heart disease, and another article showed a significant positive association!

Dr. Skrabanek further commented:

> "Risk factors have nothing to do with causes. They are risk markers, but they are neither sufficient nor necessary to explain the risk. Thus, for example, the possession of a driving licence is a risk marker for death in a car accident, marshes are a risk factor for malaria, and homosexuality a risk marker for AIDS. The knowledge of risk factors rarely, if ever, contributes to the elucidation of causal mechanisms ... It is the intimation by epidemiologists that they hold the key to the causes of diseases and their prevention which makes them overstep their brief and join the moralists in their preaching how to avoid death by being good, clean-living citizens." (193)

Not only have entire divisions of science, such as epidemiology, been subordinated to the health activists' goals, but they also habitually violate the conventions of scientific procedure and statistical analysis in order to exaggerate their case, thus undermining scientific objectivity. Professor Peter Finch, foundation professor of statistics at Monash University, Australia, observes that the health activists habitually seize on any statistical correlation, however marginal, and immediately demand political intervention by a misrepresentation of the evidence, now matter how complex the issue may really be:

> "Indeed one is forced to conclude that some health activists either lack a proper understanding of their subject or are being deliberately dishonest ... For the statistician the odd thing is that so many people are sure that complex problems have well-defined unique solutions, that scientists are the people to find them and that, as noted by C. P. Snow in his essay "Science and Government", 'Even at the highest level of decision, men do not really relish the complexity of brute reality, and they will hare after a simple concept whenever one shows its head' ... Scientific objectivity is not about the motivation for doing research, nor the source of its funding, it has to do with the criteria by which we assess it. But these criteria are being eroded by the politicisation of science, especially in matters of health.

"Health activists have contributed to this erosion of scientific standards by adopting the LaLonde doctrine that 'action has to be taken even if all the scientific evidence is not in ...'. Creative statistics includes not only selecting the facts to suit one's case and presenting them in the most advantageous way to silence opposition and induce others to adopt one's point of view, it is also based on the idea that one's perception of the world is the only correct one. Particularly in matters of human behaviour, whether it be religious observance, lifestyle or political organisation, there are always those who think that God blundered when he gave us free-will and seek to rectify that by limiting the choices available to us." (194)

It is amazing that the media has given virtually no attention to the LaLonde Doctrine. What we have here is a blatant declaration by a leading health fascist that he and his fellows are entitled to engage in the Platonic "Noble Lie", for the good of the masses of course. The LaLonde Doctrine has never been repudiated by the medical establishment. This alone should lead us to deal with all their claims with great scepticism.

No human activity could be further removed from the fundamental methods and techniques of propaganda than science. The scientific method as we understand it today is usually dated from the time of Galileo Galilei, a founder of modern empiricism, who emphasised the need to search for answers in nature rather than in the works of Aristotle. While the debate continues as to the fundamental nature of the scientific process, the analysis of the late Sir Karl Popper, the most distinguished philosopher of science of this century, is the most definitive. Sir Karl contended that scientific theories can never ultimately be proved to be true; they can only be subject to refutation in the light of new evidence. He concludes that we can therefore never be really certain about a scientific theory:

> "With the idol of certainty (including that of degrees of imperfect certainty or probability) there falls one of the defences of obscurantism which bar the way of scientific advance. For the worship of this idol hampers not only the boldness of our questions, but also the rigour and the integrity of our tests. The wrong view of science betrays itself in the craving to be right; for it is not his possession of knowledge, of irrefutable truth, that makes the man of science, but his persistent and recklessly critical quest for truth ... Science never pursues the illusory aim of making its answers final, or even probable. Its advance is, rather, towards an infinite yet attainable aim: that of ever discovering new, deeper, and more general problems, and of subjecting our ever tentative

answers to ever renewed and ever more rigorous tests." (195)

Even if we do not accept the whole Popperian approach, it is nevertheless true that a clear defining characteristic of science is its openness to objective criticism, to bold "conjecture and refutation". For the progress of science to continue, it behoves every scientist to be scrupulous in maintaining the highest standards of probity, honesty and integrity when pronouncing on subjects pertaining to his or her work. It is clear that the work of the health activists is propaganda rather than true science. They attempt to make all public discourse "one-sided", to "exclude contradiction" by both censorship or defamation and stigmatisation of critics and opponents.

The practice of various forms of deception in science is widespread and of long standing. The American writers William Broad and Nicholas Wade, in their survey of fraud and deceit in science, argue that these practices are an inevitable result of the current dependency of scientific endeavour on finance from the state:

> "Few scientists today can leave it to posterity to judge their work; their universities may deny them tenure, and the flow of grants and contracts from the federal government is likely to dry up quite quickly, unless evidence of immediate and continuing success is forthcoming." (196)

They go on to assert that:

> "The independence of science from society is important for several reasons, not least of which is that corrupt motives in one institution can often infect and distort arrangements in the other ... [T]he pathology of Lysenkoism starkly illustrates the falsifications that result when a political ideology is imposed on science. The reverse process ... is the corruption of society by false science, a disease with less conspicuous symptoms but even graver consequences. In the search for legitimacy, political ideologies often turn to science, especially to biology and the difficult issues of genetics and evolution." (197)

Lysenkoism was the pseudo-scientific doctrines of the notorious charlatan Trofim Lysenko, who came to dominate Soviet biology from the 1930s to the 1960s. Lysenko's fraudulent claims about agricultural science contradicted what scientists knew about

Darwinian evolution and Mendelian genetics. However, because these claims were more in line with Marxist-Leninist doctrine than were conventional "bourgeois" genetics, Lysenko and his followers were elevated to the highest positions of Soviet science. Those scientists who dared question Lysenko's claims were dealt with drastically. For example, Nikolai I. Vavilov, one of the world's most distinguished geneticists, who had challenged Lysenko's doctrines on strictly scientific grounds, was arrested in 1940 for allegedly spying for Britain, and died in prison in 1943, probably from malnutrition.

Although such extreme distortions of scientific procedure may seem unlikely in the West today, Broad and Wade nevertheless suggest that in order to protect the objectivity of science from political influence, "Perhaps basic scientific research would be more appropriately supported by private patrons, as economist Milton Friedman has suggested, instead of by the government." (198)

Similarly, the late Paul Feyerabend, the self-styled "epistemological anarchist", believed that scientists corrupted their essence once science started to become wrapped up in the interests of the state, and called for the divestment of "Big Science" from state support.

The Popperian philosopher the late William W. Bartley III has argued that the academic world, the "marketplace of ideas", is far less of a real market than the real marketplace of the production of goods and services. In the latter market forces and common law standards maintain real quality and a high degree of honesty. The academic world, he argues, resembles far more a feudal order. Corruption, nepotism, obscurantism, intellectual "cartels", suppression of dissent and competition, fraud, plagiarism, theft, false advertising, lies, slander, "conspiracies of silence", deceit etc are all far more common in academia than they are in business. (199) Woe betide the scholar who bucks predominant medical orthodoxy. Research funds, academic appointment or advancement are controlled by "medical barons" who will allow no threat to their favoured doctrine. I regret that the rather strict British laws of libel prevent me from elaborating further on this point.

Whether or not a separation of science and state is a realistic prospect in the current political climate in the Western world, where the state is continually extending its grip over virtually all forms of human endeavour, is highly debatable. What is vital, however, is that the honest journalist and the informed citizen must now recognise that, in the word of the late Professor Petr Beckmann, that "degrees and academics careers are no longer guarantees of honesty, truthfulness, or even competence" (200). The natural sciences have now been drawn into the political struggles of our times, and hence grievously corrupted. It is thus the responsibility of all individuals who wish to judge the merits of any political conflict into which science has been conscripted to acquaint themselves with science and scientific reasoning. There is no alternative, unless one wishes to be led by the nose into the sort statist and authoritarian order into which paternalists and collectivists have failed to dragoon us by other means.

What is indubitable is the absolute dependence of the development of the scientific endeavour on the absolute integrity of every scientist. Let us leave the last word on this topic to one of Britain's most distinguished scientists, Sir Peter Medawar, winner of the 1960 Nobel Prize for Medicine for his work on tissue transplantation:

> "The most heinous offence a scientist as a scientist can commit is to declare to be true that which is not so; if a scientist cannot interpret the phenomenon he is studying, it is a binding obligation upon him to make it possible for another to do so. If a scientist is suspected of falsifying or inventing evidence to promote his material interests or to corroborate a pet hypothesis, he is relegated to a kind of half-world separated from real life by a curtain of disbelief; for as with other human affairs, science can only proceed on a basis of confidence, so that scientists do not suspect each other of dishonesty or sharp practice, and believe each other unless there is very good reason to do otherwise." (201)

5: The Corruption of the Media

A large degree of responsibility for the spread of unfounded health scares must be laid at the door of the media, both state-owned and private. It is a regrettable fact that, throughout the Western world, the agenda of the health activists has been uncritically accepted by most of the media, which then presents both news and analysis through the filters laid down by these activists. This results in the fact that 'public opinion', as measured in opinion polls, sharply contradicts the professional opinions of risk experts. And in 'public opinion polls', of course, most of those interviewed simply repeat what they have been told by the media. Mark Mills, executive director of the Centre for Science, Technology and the Media, in Washington, DC, gives the following example:

> "A 1990 Roper and Environmental Protection Agency (EPA) study on risk found a tremendous divergence between the opinions of experts and those of the public. A list of 28 different risks was evaluated by 75 risk experts and ranked in order of seriousness. A public poll of the same risks was conducted by Roper. Not only did the two rank orderings not agree, but the rankings appeared to be virtually reversed. There was, in short, an inverse correlation between the real threat of environmental risks and public perceptions of those risks. The study found, however, a close correlation between the public ranking and media attention afforded the risks. In other words, the more attention devoted to the risk, the more the public perceived the risk as a serious threat to themselves." (202)

Many specialist correspondents and members of the media, with a few honourable exceptions, are lazy and thus happy to be fed press releases by lobby groups (at least, the "politically correct" ones). Some are intellectually second rate, and unable to understand technical, criticisms of simplistic propaganda (Oh the stories we could tell!). Some are explicit ideological allies of the health activists, and work hand in glove with them to maximise the effectiveness of their campaigns and to stifle or discredit any opposition. Many just share the assumptions of the "New Class", that paternalism is justified, that the only businessmen – and not scientists, health activists or bureaucrats – have vested interests.

Professor Vincent Marks, who is both professor of clinical biochemistry at the University of Surrey, Guildford, and head of the department of clinical biochemistry and nutrition at the Royal Surrey County Hospital, Guildford, is highly critical of the attitude of much of the media towards scientists whose scientific findings contradict the entrenched myths of the health activists:

"Some of the most notorious of today's hucksters have the effrontery to accuse scientists whose work is of the highest ethical and internationally recognised standards, but of whom they disapprove, as being in the pocket of those who fund their research. The intention is to make such workers appear unreliable and untrustworthy witnesses. This attempt by the apocalyptics and unscrupulous to divert attention away from the real issues is similar to that used by the pickpocket to distract the attention of his victim whilst relieving him of his wallet. In this game of character assassination it is generally not the quality of the scientist's work that the hucksters attack – since this is often beyond reproach – but the investigator's personal integrity. This sort of behaviour, which has no bearing on the subject matter under discussion, is anathema to scientists and similarly reputable people. It is, however, commonplace among gutter journalists and others who work on the basis that if you throw mud, some of it will stick.

"I, for example, was reviled in the press when I first described, under the title of "Muesli Belt Malnutrition", a condition resulting from the imposition upon young children by their overly anxious, usually middle-class, literate, but misguided mothers, of feeding regimes that were totally unsuitable for them. I was accused of being in the pay (pocket) of the sugar industry, the confectionery industry or even the food industry as a whole, as though the only possible reason for exposing problems caused by ignorance is financial." (203)

On another occasion, Professor Marks gave a talk on the nutritional aspects of sugar at a public meeting:

"I concluded then, as now, that 'there is very little convincing evidence that increased consumption of sugar (sucrose) is really responsible, in the population as a whole, for producing any disease apart from caries of the teeth...' I was reported, however, as saying that sugar in the diet causes disease." (204)

It is hardly surprising, given Professor Marks's experience, that journalists, including those in the 'quality' press, give prominent coverage to the most outlandish claims by the health activists. Now most of these well-publicised health scares do not even last long enough to warrant the label of "nine-day wonders". However, because there is a regrettable tendency among both the public and members of the political class – most of whom lack even the most cursory knowledge of the scientific process – to "read by headline". Thus, a climate of opinion is created which is favourable to ever-increasing regulation and legislation from Brussels, Whitehall and Westminster. There is a small but growing literature on the political corruption of science, and on the political agenda of "health fascism", but it is still miniscule and underfunded in comparison with the health fascist lobbies and with the scientific and medical establishment in general. The Social Affairs Unit has done some stirling work and produced some fine papers, but much of the remaining literature is American or non-British, and difficult to obtain. (205)

6: The Puerility of the Business Response

Given the portrayal defamation of critics of the health activists as mercenary lackeys of the various "barons", and the portrayal of capitalists as powerful and devious lobbyists, the truth of the matter is doubly ironic.

In reality, virtually every business response to attack is inept and pathetic. Most businesses engage in pre-emptive cringing, and lean over backwards to be "reasonable". Instead of confronting, refuting and defeating their enemies they produce platitudes. They have no conception of the nature of the opposition they face, an opposition which is determined to destroy or cripple them. They "compromise", when compromises only encourage their opponents, further undermine their own case, and open the door to the next restriction. They rely on sleazy PR hacks who have no understanding of the power of political ideologies and movements and no idea how to combat them. They think things can be sorted out with behind-the-scenes words or "deals" with politicians – politicians who cannot be trusted and will succumb to whoever exerts the most pressure. And the reality is that a few lobbyists' lunches with politicians, and a few donations to the funds of political parties, are as nothing compared to the force of a fanatical, "idealistic", and well-organised political campaign. Industry thus wastes money on puerile PR which achieves nothing but lining the pockets of incompetent and usually cynical PR companies.

The pattern has been repeated in industry after industry. At the present time the alcohol industry funds a fatuous organisation called "The Portman Group", which provides no principled opposition to their enemies, but postures as an embodiment of "responsibility" and rectitude. Its visibility as a defender of freedom for drinkers and the industry that caters for them is virtually non-existent. And it has zero effect on the growing anti-alcohol lobby.

Indeed, some members of the alcohol industry seem to have no inkling of what is going on now, and what is in store for them in the future.

Thus, at a reception in the House of Commons sponsored by Whitbread on Tuesday 23 January 1995, two MP's researchers asked one Simon Ward, the Strategic Affairs Director for Whitbread plc what exactly his firm was doing to confront the growing threat. He dismissed both sets of warnings, stated that he "saw no problems whatsoever" for his industry, and boasted that sales were not currently decreasing. He dismissed the idea that there was any similarity at all between the campaigns against the tobacco industry and the campaigns against his own. Some strategy! The shareholders should certainly ask what someone with such political myopia is doing as their "Strategic (sic) Affairs" Director.

The food industry seems similarly inept. D. M. Conning, Director-General of The British Nutrition Foundation, has publicly criticised the "feeble attempt at appeasement by manufacturers under attack". (206) A classic example was "Healthy Eating: Time for Action!", a one day conference at the Royal Society of Medicine supported by the Department of Health. The Conference was intended to promote the health fascist programme announced by the Nutrition Task Force, to "[get] the message on Health Eating across to consumers". Yet members of United Biscuits, Sainsburys and Nestles, Lucas Ingredients and others participated as speakers, alongside their dedicated enemies in the HEA, the Task Force, and other health fascist groups.

At the moment the food industry is wavering with the idea of accepting "voluntary guidelines", blind to the disaster that these have been for the tobacco industry. To accept them would to open the door to a ceaseless onslaught of further restrictions and regulation.

Even the Advertising Association has come out in support of the Health of the Nation targets. (207) But advertising is the principal target of every health fascist and anti-business campaign. The destruction of commercial free speech, advertising, is absolutely essential if the propaganda of health fascism is to fully effective. And the health fascists know this if the advertising industry doesn't. The Advertising Association, of all people should clearly say that it is not the role of government to mould the lifestyles and choices of its citizens, that censorship in any form is unacceptable, and that they are not going to co-operate in the cutting of their own throats. By making such a concession to the "Health of the Nation", they have thus undercut any principled argument they could make against their opponents. By throwing away principle they are thus left with only "pragmatic" arguments about exactly how much of their business will be destroyed. Their enemies will churn out ever more pseudo-science, bogus arguments and phony statistics about the allegedly overwhelming power of advertising and the need to control it. One would have thought that the lessons of the pre-War appeasement of the Nazis would have established for all time the lesson that deadly foes cannot be appeased. But apparently not.

The idea that defenders of free choice and a free economy can rely on generous financial or any other sort of support from business interests has proved laughable. The freedom of consumers and the freedom of businesses to serve them will be saved, if at all, without the support of the latter. The fact that the corrupters of science and the enemies of liberty have privileged access to both the media and to the financial largesse of the State (i.e., the taxapayer) thus means that the struggle for scientific objectivity and political liberty will be a long and difficult one.

7: The Moral and Political Critique

The fundamental case against health fascism and its health scares is, of course, a moral and political one. It is re-assertion of the liberal view that individuals are autonomous agents with free will, and not mindless zombies helpless before the forces of advertising, social or any other sort of conditioning. One could cite much empirical evidence on the effects of advertising, to show that it does not possess the miraculous powers attributed to it by its critics. But this is really gratuitous. Introspection and simple observation alone demonstrate the existence of free will and autonomy, although more sophisticated philosophical and psychological works add to our understanding. (208)

As the always perceptive journalist Minette Marin has put it:

> "The flight from personal responsibility is probably the central moral phenomenon of the late- 20th century. If your toddler drowns, while unattended, in his own nappy bucket, clearly, according to conventional wisdom, the Government must do something about nappy buckets, and pass a law or something. If your child drowns, while unattended, in a DIY garden pool, there must be a large official warning on all garden pool kits, not to mention a support group and counselling for all concerned. This is the message of Radio 4, and other concerned and caring bodies. The Government, or somebody, must be blamed, or if all else fails, one's parents and their secret crimes ...

It may just be another faith about to fail, but there is a belief central to any civilised society that the individual is responsible for his actions. Of course there is room for understanding and compassion, of course there are mitigating circumstances, but to dump one's guilt on someone or something else is infantile.

When a culture abandons individual responsibility, which is to say the self's power over the self, it leaves a power vacuum that someone else will be quick to fill. Someone else will take control over the individual. That way lies totalitarianism. I cannot understand why people are not more afraid of it." (209)

There can be no compromise in the struggle against health fascism. Either individuals are, in John Locke's words, "proprietors over their own selves", or they are wards of the state. Once one allows dictation to the individual "for their own good", there is no limit to tyranny. And, of course, the good of people is almost always the justification tyrants give for tyranny. Indeed as the great American judge Louis D. Brandeis declared in 1928, "Experience teaches us to be most on our guard to protect liberty when the government's purposes are beneficent ... The greatest dangers to liberty lurk in insidious encroachment by men of zeal, well-meaning but without understanding". To what extent the motives of the health fascists are really "well-meaning" might be disputed. H. L. Mencken's more cynical view that "The urge to save humanity is almost always a false front for the urge to rule" might be nearer to the truth.

The evasiveness of the health fascists, their general unwillingness to admit that their agenda is a coercive one, the way they deny that their policies of censorship and the mobilisation of both public and private bodies in the "struggle for health" is anything other than totalitarian, says a lot about their honesty. It perhaps gives us glimpse into the intensity of their urge to rule.

Health Fascism and state paternalism are a reactionary reversion to a more primitive stage of society. The similarity with, for example, the religious paternalism and persecution that deformed so much of European history is striking. Today few are concerned with the welfare of their, or others', souls. In a secular age the primary concern is with the material. And those who believe they are endowed with truth and virtue see it as their right to preserve the bodily, rather than spiritual, welfare of others, whether those others like it or not! But the "saving" of souls or bodies by the use of state coercion and censorship is an absolute evil, an affront to true morality, and at war with all decency, all justice, and our inalienable human rights.

Notes

1. Chris R. Tame, *Non-Smokers Unite ...,* FOREST, London, 1995

2. Jacques Ellul, *Propaganda*, [first published 1962], translated by Konrad Kellen and Jean Lerner, Vintage Books/Random House, New York, 1973 edition, page 7.

3. *ibid*, page 11.

4. *ibid*, pages 17-18.

5. *ibid*, page 25.

6. *ibid*, pages 30-31.

7. *ibid*, page 38.

8. *ibid*, page 47.

9. Quoted in James Le Fanu, "A Healthy Diet – Fact or Fashion?" in Peter Berger et al, *Health, Lifestyle and Environment: Countering the Panic*, Social Affairs Unit/Manhattan Institute, London, 1991, p. 90. See also James L. Fanu, *A Phantom Carnage: The Myth That Low Income Kills*, Social Affairs Unit, London, 1993, for a critique of more modern versions of this sort of approach.

10. *ibid*, p. 93.

11. *ibid*, p. 103.

12. Quoted in Robert Browning, "Who Are the Health Activists?", in Peter Berger et al, *Health, Lifestyle and Environment*, Op Cit, p. 37.

13. Catherine Montgomery Blight and Simon Scanlan, "Regulating Cakes and Ale", in Digby Anderson, ed., *A Diet of Reason: Sense and Nonsense in the Healthy Eating Debate*, Social Affairs Unit, London, 1986, pp. 136, 137.

14. Marks, *Is British Food Bad for You?*, IEA Health & Welfare Unit, London, 1991, p. 3.

15. Donald J. McNamara, "Diet and Heart Disease", in Anderson, *A Diet of Reason, op. cit.*, page 41.

16. Digby Anderson, "Healthy Eating: The Evidence", in *ibid*, p. 14. For a longer study of food panics see Elizabeth Whelan & Frederick J. Stare, *Panic In the Pantry: Facts and Fallacies About the Food You Buy* [1975], 2nd edn., Prometheus Books, Buffalo, New York, 1993 and Idem, *The One-Hundred-Percent Natural, Purely Organic, Cholesterol-Free, Megavitamin, Low-Carbohydrate Nutrition Hoax,* Atheneum, New York, 1983.

17. Chronicles, 14(5), May 1990, p. 48.

18. Thomas Prentice, "Risk from Low-Fat Diet is Challenged", *The Times*, 8 April, 1985.

19. Marks, Is British Food Bad for You?, *op. cit.*, p. 13.

20. Barbara Pickard, "Dairy Products and Red Meat" in Anderson, *A Diet of Reason, op. cit.*, pages 21-22.

21. Quoted in *ibid*, p. 22.

22. Quoted in *ibid*, p. 22.

23. *ibid*, p. 23.

24. Quoted in *ibid*, p. 34.

25. Quoted in *The Daily Telegraph*, magazine section, 4th June 1992.

26. Quoted in *ibid*.

27. McNamara, *op. cit.*, pp. 48-49.

28. Pickard, *op. cit.*, p. 36-37.

29. Amongst a large and growing critical literature, see A. K. Armitage, ed., *Other People's Tobacco Smoke*, Galen Press, Beverley, East Yorkshire, 1991; Domingo M. Aviado, MD, "Health Issues Relating to 'Passive Smoking'", in Robert D. Tollison, ed., *Smoking and Society: Toward a More Balanced Assessment*, Lexington Books/D. C. Heath, Lexington, Mass., 1986; Donald J. Ecobichon and Joseph M. Wu, eds., *Environmental Tobacco Smoke: Proceedings of the International Symposium at McGill University*, 1989, Lexington Books/D. C. Heath, Lexington, Mass., 1990; Prof. Antony Flew, *Passive Smoking, Scientific Method and the Corruption of Science*, FOREST, London, 1994; Dr. Jane G. Gravelle & Dr. Dennis Zimmerman, "Statement on Environmental Tobacco Smoke to The Subcommittee on Clean Air and Nuclear Regulation Committee on Environment and Public Works of the United States Senate", Congressional Research Service, The Library of Congress, Washington, D.C., 11 May, 1994; Dr. Gary Huber et al, "Passive Smoking: How Great a Hazard?", *Consumers' Research*, Vol. 74. No. 7, July 1991. Also reprinted as FOREST Information Sheet No. 5, FOREST, London, 1993; Dr. Gary Huber et al, "Passive Smoking and Your Heart", *Consumers' Research*, Vol. 75, No. 4, April, 1992. Also reprinted as FOREST Information Sheet No. 6, FOREST, London, 1993; Dr. Gary Huber et al, "Smoke and Mirrors: The EPA's Flawed Study of Environmental Tobacco Smoke and Lung Cancer", *Regulation* (Cato Institute Review of Business and Government), No. 3, 1993, pp. 44-54; H. Kasuga,

Environmental Tobacco Smoke, Springer-Verlag, Berlin, 1993; Peter N. Lee, *Environmental Tobacco Smoke and Mortality: A Detailed Review of the Epidemiological Evidence Relating ETS to the Risk of Cancer, Heart Disease and Other Causes of Death in Adults Who Have Never Smoked*, S. Karger AG, Basel, 1992. Chris Tame's *The Myth of Passive Smoking: A Selected Critical Bibliography*, FOREST, London, 1995, and regularly updated, provides a more comprehensive bibliography.

30. "Battle for Bacon and Eggs", *The Times*, 13 March 1994, p. 15.

31. Nigel Hawkes, "Hole in the Heart of the Cholesterol Cult", *The Times*, 21 October 1991)

32. Nigel Hawkes, "The Cholesterol Scare Has Been Overplayed", *The Times*, 10 January 1996, p. 13.

33. Nigel Hawkes, "An Out-of-Date View of Diet", *The Times*, 16 November, 1993.

34. *Nigel Hawkes, "Will a Fruit and Vegetable Diet Make You Live Longer?", The* Times, 16 May 1995, p. 15. Other contributions by Hawkes on this issue can be found in: "Funeral for a High-Fad Diet?, *The Times*, 28 February, 1991; "Leaving Us to Our Chips: This Hectoring Is Even Worse", *The Times*, 22 September, 1991; "You Are What They Ate", The Times Saturday Review, 6 June 1992, pp. 10-12. Although outbalanced by presentations of the cholesterol establishment there has been a degree of press coverage of dissenting views. See Ann Kent, "A Fat Lot of Good", *The Times*, 13 September, 1990; Jane E. Brody, "Skepticism on Low-Fat Diets", *International Herald Tribune*, 27 Jume 1991; William Langley, "Proof That You Can Eat, Drink, Be Merry – and Live Longer", *The Evening Standard*, 1 May 1992, p. 21; Jeremy Laurence, "Low-Fat Diet Advice to Women is Wrong, Heart Study Finds", *The Times*, 16 April 1993; Vernon Coleman, "Second Opinion: The Fat Question", *What Doctors Don't Tell You*, 3(12), 1993, p. 8.

35. James Le Fanu, *Eat Your Heart Out: The Fallacy of the Healthy Diet*, Macmillan, London, 1987.

36. *ibid*, pp. 168, 153, 155.

37. U. Ravnskov, "Cholesterol Lowering Trials in Coronary Heart Disease: Frequency of Citation and Outcome", *British Medical Journal*, Vol. 305, 4 July 1992, p. 19.

38. Robert Matthews, "Stay Fat and Keep Healthy, Say US

Scientists", *The Sunday Telegraph*, 12 June 1994.

39. J. D. Swales, "Salt and High Blood Pressure", in *A Diet of Reason*, Op Cit, p. 53.

40. Quoted in *ibid*, p. 54.

41. Quoted in *ibid*, p. 54.

42. *ibid*, p. 66.

43. *The Lancet*, Vol. 11, 1984, p. 436.

44. James Le Fanu, "For 'Mass Prevention' Read 'Mass Con'", *New Scientist*, 105, 29 March 1985, p. 43.

45. Ian Macdonald, "Fibre", *Diet of Reason, op. cit.*, pp. 69, 75-76.

46. Quoted in Marks, "Exploding the Myths About Sugar", *ibid*, p. 8.

47. Marshall Midda, "Dental Caries and the Conscientious Consumer", in *ibid*, p. 92.

48. Quoted in *ibid*, p. 93.

49. Marks, Is British Food Bad for You?, *op. cit.*, p. 22.

50. This story, as is typical of the way in which the health fascist network operates with its media allies, was also vigorously pushed in a Channel 4 "Dispatches" documentary programme.

51. *A Diet of Reason, op. cit.*, p. 20.

52. *ibid*, pp. 27-28.

53. Dr. James Le Fanu, "The Guerilla War Mankind Can't Win", *The Sunday Telegraph*, 12 February 1989.

54. Richard North and Teresa Gorman, *Chickengate: An Independent Analysis of the Salmonella in Eggs Scare*, Health Unit Paper No. 10, Health & Welfare Unit, Institute of Economic Affairs, London, 1990.

55. *ibid*, p. 114.

56. Richard North & Christopher Booker, "Curse of the Regulator", *The Sunday Telegraph*, 27 June 1993, p. 19

57. See Richard North and Christopher Booker, *The Mad Officials*, ... 1995

58. "Fowl Play", Time Out, 25 May-1 June 1994, p. 29

59. Marks, Is British Food Bad For You, *op. cit.*, p. 31.

60. "Time to Stop Milking This Mad Cow Hysteria", *The Daily Telegraph*, 22 May, 1990.

61. *ibid*, p. 23. And see also Glenn G. Lamni, There They Go Again: Activists Use Junk Science to Block Food Irradiation Technology, *Legal Opinion Letter*, Washington Legal Foundation, Washington,

DC, 1992.

62. See "Editorial: Food and Hysteria", *Wall Street Journal*, 28 April, 1994, p. 6.

63. *Labour Briefing*, July 1994, p. 12.

64. *Labour Briefing*, February 1995, pp. 12-13

65. "Fight the Big Mac", *Counter Information*, No. 43, August-October, 1995, p. 2.

66. And see also "Making NcDonald's Ear Their Words", *Labour Briefing*, September 1995, p. 21; "Fast Food, Slow Trial", *The Journalist*, Jume/July 1995, pp. 16-17; "Burger Bosses Battered", *The Law*, March-May 1995, pp. 14-15; Pat Turnbull, "More Than Beef in Thse Hamburgers", *Straight Left*, September, 1994, p. 3; Richard Woods, "Fast-Food Giant Slowly Nibbling at the Greens", *The Sunday Times*, 12 March, 1995.

67. "McLibel", *Organise!* (Anarchist Communist Federation), No,. 28, October-December 1992, p. 7.

68. See "Campaigners Defy McLiers", *Labour Briefing*, May 1994, p. 5.

69. See "Kings Cross McProtest", *Camden New Journal*, 14 December 1995, p. 2.

70. "Ex-US Surgeon General Lays Into Fat", *International Herald Tribune*, 7 December 1994, p. 7.

71. Quoted in *Your Freedom*, No. 7, August 1994, p. 7.

72. Ann Kent, "How Many Food Nannies Make a Healthy Nation", *The Times*, 11 October, 1990.

73. Geoffrey Cannon, "Battle for the British Diet", *The Sunday Times*, 3 July 1983.

74. "Letter", *The Times*, Magazine, 18 March 1995, p. 6.

75. Geoffrey Canon, "Soapbox: Food Advertisers Resort to Tricks of Tobacco Trade", *Marketing Magazine*, 4 May 1995, p. 14.

76. Joe-Suamamrez Smith, "Health Lobby Targets Chocs on the Box", *The Sunday Telegraph*, 5 February, 1995, p. 17.

77. *ibid.*

78. See "Food Industry Targeted", *Ad Issues*, Advertising Association, London, January 1995, pp. 1-2. This case is similar to the so-called Smee Report, produced by an anti-smoking lobby fellow-traveller in the Department of Health, and similarly demolished by informed economic analysis. See John C. Luik, ed.,

Do Tobacco Advertising Bans Really Work?, The Niagara Institute, Ontario, 1994.

79. Ad Issues, Op Cit, p. 2.

80. Tom Kemp, "A Father Writes ... Health Lessons From the Enemy Within", *The Daily Telegraph*, 15 December, 1995, p. 21

81. Judy Jones, "Let Them Eat Cake, But Don't Let Them Win", *The Observer*, 14 August, 1994, p. 19. Just one earlier example of a smear campaign against criticism can be found in the *The Lancet* in 1983, when it accused the food industry of trying to suppress a Department of Health Report; "Lancet Attacks Diet 'Cover Up'", *The Sunday Times*, 7 August 1983. Again, we find experts attempting to sweep dissent under the scientific carpet. Sir Richard Turner, a Senior Research Fellow in Preventive Cardiology, thus asserted that there is "practically a universal consensus of opinion throughout the world, as to what constitutes a health diet". He attacked the food industry, and called for the press to play a "vital role" in the campaign, ie, to transform itself into an even more obsequious transmitter of propaganda to mobilise the masses into obedience to the diktats of the gauleiters of health. "Can We Survive Our Diet?", *The Sunday Times*, 7 August, 1983.

82. "Menu for the Masses Unveiled", *The Sunday Telegraph*, 7 August, 1994.

83. Liz Hunt, "Are We Sitting Too Comfortably?", *The Independent*, 3 October 1995, p. 15.

84. See, for example, "Food Advisors Links 'Hidden'", *The Guardian*, 12 May 1993, p. 7.

85. See Dianna Simmons, "Consuming Interests: Health", *City Limits*, 3-9 May, 1983.

86. See Josephine Fairley, "Safety on the Menu", *The Times*, 23 March 199?.

87. See Eliot Marshal, "A is for Apple, Alar ... Alarmism", *Science*, 4 October 1991. And see Chris R. Tame, *"Junk Science" in Action: Notes on the Environmental Protection Agency*, FOREST, London, 19??, pp. 6-7 for a brief critique and for more references to the critical literature of the Alar hoax.

88. See "Letters", *The Guardian*, 20 March 1991.

89. See Colin Spencer, "Better Safe Than Never", *The Guardian*, Weekend Supplement, 2-3 June, 1990, p. 23.

90. See Jad Adams, "The Guilty Bug", *i to i*, No. 2, February 1990,

p. 23. Adams is one of the few writers to recognise and describe how "Food is one of the areas to which the left retreated in its decade of decline in the 1980's. The rhetoric of the left and the stance of the left is adopted by the food campaigners".

91. Angela Neustatter, "Powers of Persuasion", *The Guardian*, 10 October 1990.

92. Kathryn Knight, "Health Profits on Low-Fat Foods", *The Times*, 19 October, 1994, p. 6.

93. Judy Sadgrove, "Some People: Ian Munro, The Thunderer at *The Lancet*", *The Guardian*, 1 November 1988. See the contributions by Munro in the CPGB publication *News & Views*, August 1988, p. 21, and in *Changes*, Supplement, 20 July – 2 August, 1991, pp. 3-4.

94. "Consumer Council Presses for Charter to Ensure Food Safety", *The Times*, 15 March 1989, p. 6.

95. "Fatty Diets Leaves Young Short of Nutrients", The Times, 2 March, 1994.

96. "Food Label Shortcomings 'Cost 500 Lives a Week'" The Guardian, 27 March 1992.

97. See Nigel Hawkes, "The Cholesterol Scare Has Been Overplayed", *The Times*, 10 January 1996, p. 13.

98. Juliet Rix, "A Massage From Our Sponsor", *The Guardian*, 22 April, 1992.

99. Douglas Jay, *The Socialist Case*, Victor Gollancz, London, 1947, p. 258.

100. J. C. Dr.ummond and Anne Wilbraham, *The Englishman's Food: A History of Five Centuries of English Diet*, originally published by Jonathan Cape, London, 1939; & rev edn, 1957; reprinted by Pimlico, London, 1991.

101. *ibid*, p. 462.

102. Quoted in Aileen Ballantyne, "Life-Giving Legacy of the War", *The Times*, 2 February 1993, p. 14.

103. Marya Burgess, "Down in the Mouth", *The Guardian*, Weekend Supplement, 29-30 September 1990, p. 19

104. "Your Say in the Food Chain", *The Guardian*, Weekend Supplement, March 3-4, 1990.

105. See *Civil Abolitionist*, 7(2), 1995, on the American campaign re USDA guidelines.

106. *The Times*, 24 June 1994, p. 4.

107. Tony Banks MP, "Eat Your Greens", *New Times*, 18 March 1995, p. 5.

108. See John Sutherland, "Beware of Proselytizing Vegetarians", *Gauntlet*, No. 3, 1992, pp. 118-119 & Julia Llewellyn Smith, "Tyranny of the Veggies", *The Times*, 28 January 1994, p. 12.

109. Brett Silverstein, *Fed Up! The Food Forces That Make You Fat, Sick and Poor*, South End Press, Boston, Mass, 1995.

110. Richard Lacey, *Unfit For Human Consumption: Food in Crisis – The Consequences of Putting Profit Before Safety*, Souvenir Books, London, 1991. And see also *Hard to Swallow: A Brief History of Food*, Cambridge University Press, 1994.

111. Libby Purvess, "Brown Rice With a Serving of Cant", *The Times*, 7 December 1990, p. 18, writing about *Greenscene*, Vegetarian Society magazine aimed at children.

112. Carol J. Adams, *The Sexual Politics of Meat: A Feminist Vegetarian Critical Theory*, Polity Press, Cambridge, 1990.

113. *ibid*, pp. 190, 54, 29.

114. Colin Spencer's *The Heretics Feast: A History of Vegetarianism*, Fourth Estate, London, 1993.

115. Deane W. Curtin and Lisa M. Heldke, eds., *Cooking, Eating, Thinking: Transformative Philosophies of Food*, Indiana University Press, Bloomington, 1996.

116. Michael Prowse, "Why Vegetarians Will Inherit the Earth", *The Financial Times,* 11 July 1994, p. 16.

117. Dr. Thomas Stuttaford, "The Benefits of Moderate Drinking", in Digby Anderson, ed., *Drinking to Your Health*, Social Affairs Unit, London, 1989, pp. 29, 31.

118. Quoted in *The Daily Telegraph*, magazine section, 4th June 1992.

119. Stuttaford, *ibid*, p. 34.

120. *ibid*, p. 37. And see also the more recent studies, Digby Anderson, *Take a Little Wine – or Beer or Whisky – For Your Stomach's Sake: Alcohol Research and Alcohol Policy*, Social Affairs Unit, London, 1995 and Morris Chafetz E. & D. Marion, *Drink Moderately and Live Longer: Understanding the Good of Alcohol*, 1995

121. Quoted in P. M. Jackson, "Estimating the Social Costs of Alcohol Abuse", in *ibid*, pp. 72-73.

122. A. M. Cooper, "How Different Societies Learn to Drink", in

ibid, p. 211.

123. Kurt Hellman, "Alcohol: A Carcinogenic Risk", in ibid, pp. 166, 169.

124. Quoted in Dwight B. Heath, "Policies, Politics and Pseudo-science", in Anderson, ed., *Drinking to Your Health, op. cit.*, p. 39.

125. Quoted in ibid, p. 39.

126. Quoted in *ibid*, p. 40.

127. Quoted in *ibid*, p. 39.

128. See Douglas J. Den Uyl, "Smoking, Human Rights, and Civil Liberties", "Appendix 6A: The Political Philosophy of the World Health Organization", in Robert D. Tollison, Smoking and Society: Toward a More Balanced Assessment, Lexington Books/D. C. Heath, Lexington, Mass., 1986, pp. 214-215.

129. Quoted in Drinking To Your Health, p. 43.

130. Quoted in Douglas Mason, *Time to Call Time*, Adam Smith Institute, London, 1986, p. 9.

131. Quoted in *ibid*, p. 10.

132. Quoted in *ibid*, p. 10.

133. Quoted in Charles Plouviez, "Food Advertising Not the Problem", in Anderson, *A Diet of Reason, op. cit.*, p. 127.

134. Quoted in M. J. Waterson, "Advertising and Alcohol", in Anderson, *Drinking to Your Health, op. cit.*, p. 113.

135. Quoted in Heath, *op. cit.*, p. 48.

136. *ibid*, p. 50.

137. "Ban All Drink Advertising", *The Daily Telegraph*, 27 June, 1985.

138. See Hugh Bayley, "When Doctor Doesn't Know Best", *The New Statesman*, 27 October, 1995, p. 20 and Andrew Long & Stephen Harrison, "The Balance of Evidence", *Health Service Journal: Health Management Guide*, Supplement Issue No. 6, 1995, pp. 1-2 and "An ABC of Evidence", pp. 3-11. On the dangers of contemporary established medical usage see Martin Weitz*, Health Shock: A Guide to Ineffective and Hazardous Medical Treatment*, David & Charles, Newton Abboy, 1980 and Dr. Robert S. Mendelsohn, *Confessions of a Medical Heretic*, Warner Books, New York, 1979.

139. Quoted in *The Sunday Telegraph*, 23rd June 1991.

140. Quoted in *ibid.*

141. On the background to medical paternalism and health fascism in Britain see: Michael Freeden, "Eugenics and Progressive Thought: A Study in Ideological Affinity", *Historical Journal*, Vol. 22, No. 3, 1979; Greta Jones, *Social Darwinism and English Thought: The Interaction Between Biological and Social Theory*, The Harvester Press, Brighton, East Sussex, 1980; Greta Jones, *Social Hygiene in Twentieth Century Britain*, Croom Helm, London, 1986; G. R. Searle, *Eugenics and Politics in Britain 1900-1914*, Noordhoff International Publishing, Leyden, 1976; Richard A. Soloway, *Eugenics and the Declining Birthrate in Twentieth Century Britain*, The University of North Carolina Press, Chapel Hill and London, 1990. On the medical profession and its role in health fascism in Nazi Germany see the classic study by Robert Proctor, *Racial Hygiene: Medicine Under the Nazis*, Harvard University Press, Cambridge, Mass., 1988. And see also Paul Weindling, *Health, Race and German Politics Between National Unification and Nazism, 1870-1945*, Cambridge University Press, 1989 and Sheila Faith Weiss, *Race Hygiene and National Efficiency: The Eugenics of Wilhelm Schallmayer*, University of California, Los Angeles.

142. Quoted in J. A. N. Corsellis, "Boxing and the Brain", *British Medical Journal*, Volume 298, 14th January 1989, p. 108.

143. Arthur Chandler, "Banish Boxing From the Box", *Labour Briefing*, November 1991, p. 29.

144. David Fletcher, "Doctors Seek Ban on Boxing", *The Daily Telegraph*, 8 July, 1982.

145. Quoted in *The Doctor*, 5 August 1992

146. Mary Midgley, "Analysis", *The Guardian*, September 24 1991.

147. *The Guardian*, date not recored.

148. *The Doctor*, 12th August 1982.

149. Quoted in *The Doctor*, 29th July 1982.

150. See Mark Thornton, *The Economics of Prohibition*, University of Utah Press, Salt Lake City, 1991.

151. *The Doctor*, 29 July 1982.

152. Jeremy Laurance, "Doctors Urge Amateurs to Box On", *The Times*, 7 October 1993, p. 3.

153. Simon Jenkins, "The Lesson of the Benn v. McClellan Fight: Bring Back Bare-Knuckle Boxing", *The Spectator*, 4 March, 1995,

p. 32.

154. *ibid.*

155. The TV producer David Graham deals with similar moral and cultural significance of professional wrestling in *The Popular Culture of Liberalism*, Cultural Notes No. 19, Libertarian Alliance, London, 1989.

156. Simin Heffer, "Editorial: This Sporting Death", *The Spectator*, 7 May, 1994, p. 5.

157. "Letters", *The Times*, 11 July 1995, p. 17.

158. Quoted in *The Sunday Times*.

159. *The Independent.*

160. Craig Brown, "Pouring Out the Whines", *The Evening Stanadard*, 20 February, 1995, p. 11.

161. Charles Laurence, "Smell Police Are in the Sniff", *The Daily Telegraph*, 28 February 1995, p. 17. The second quote is from James Bovard, "Get a Whiff of This!", *The Wall Street Journal*, 27 December, 1995, p. 10

162. *The Philip Morris Magazine*, Spring, 1992, p. 20.

163. *The Freeview*, Hong Kong, February 1995, p. 1.

164. Susan Ellicott, "Chanel's Number May Be Up in America's Perfume Purges", *The Sunday Times*, 16 May, 1993, p. I.23.

165. Judy Sadgrove, ""Breast Implants", *Marie Clare*, February 1995, p. 133.

166. Virginia I. Postrel, "Policy Bust", *Reason*, 23(10), March 1992, p. 4.

167. David Sharrock, "Safety Concerns .. ", *The Guardian*, 7 January 1992. And see also, Michael Fumento (November 1995), "A Confederacy of Boobs", *Reason*; Virginia Postrel, (January 1996), "Abreast of History", *Reason*, 27(8), pp. 4-5

168. "Study Begins Into Video Games Risk", *The National*, No. 2, Summer 1993, p. 2.

169. "Letters", *The Times*, 29 September, 1993, p. 19

170. *The Carolina Critic*, 5(4), 15 October, 1991, p. 2.

171. See Martin Barker, *A Haunt of Fears: The Strange History of the British Horror Comic Campaign*, Pluto Press, London, 1984, and Idem, ed., *The Video Nasties: Freedom and Censorship in the Media*, Pluto Press, London, 1984. Both works are unfortunately marred by the author's Marxism.

172. In a paper delivered to the British Psychology Society Conference, quoted in "Games 'Do Not Cause Aggression'", *The Times*, Interface supplement, 20 Decmber 1995, p. 3; "Computer Games: Harmfully Addictive or a Unique Educational Environment?: An Interview With Dr. David Deutsch", The Lose Network: A Newsletter for London Out-of-School Education, No. 4, January 1993. p. 5.

173. Dr. Petr Beckmann, ""Causality" and "Death By Cellular Telephone", *Access to Energy,*. 20(7), pp. 1-2. For a longer treatment see his, *Electromagnetic Fields and VDT-itis*, The Golem Press, Boulder Colorado, 1991. And also see William Bennett, Jr., "Power Lines Are Homely, Not Dangerous", *Wall Street Journal*, 10 August 1994, p. A10 and *Health and Low-Frequency Electromagnetic Fields*, Yale University Press, 1994; Michael Fumento, "Fear of Phoning", Reason, 25(2), June 1993, pp. 52-53 and "Shock Journalism: The Junk Reporting Behind the Power Line-Cancer Connection", Reason 26(8), January 1995, pp. 23-29; H. E. Payne, *Electromagnetic Field From Utility Power Lines and Salem Witch-craft*, Payne Engineering, Scott Depot, West Virginia, 1995 (Rt. 29, Rocky Step Road, Scott Depot, West Virgina 25560, USA); Richard F. Sanford, "Shocking Distortions Versus the Current Truth on Electromagnetic Fields", SOS. Alert (Society for Objective Science), 2(1), January 1994.
The fear of electro-magnetic fields can be compared profitably with the 19th century scare in America against electricity itself. See Petr Beckmann, *Pages From US Energy History*, The Golem Press, Boulder, Colorado, 1978.

174. See David Fletcher, "Power Line Cancer Dismissed by Study", *The Daily Telegraph*, 26 August 1994; *Skeptical Inquirer*, September/October 1995, p. 4.

175. Dr. Simon Wesley, "Annoying Dose of Doubts", *The Times*, 14 July 1994, p. 17.

176. *ibid.*

177. Keith Waterhouse, "Filter-Tip of the Iceberg", *The Daily Mirror*, 24 April 1986.

178. See Professor Germy Shaper, of the British Heart Foundation, warning about coronary heart disease in 1994, in Richard Woodman, "A Damning Report ... ", *The Daily Mail*, 5 July, 1994, p. 44.

179. See Dr. Stephen Davies, *The Historical Origins of Health*

Fascism, FOREST, London, 1991.

180. See B. Bruce-Riggs, ed., *The New Class*, Transaction Books, New Brunswick, New Jersey, 1979; Nigel Ashford, *Neo-Conservatism and the New Class: A Critical Evaluation*, Cultural Notes No. 3, Libertarian Alliance, London, 1986. A brief but brilliant essay on the nature of the intellegentsia is Hans-Herman Hoppe's, *Natural Elites, Intellectuals and the State*, Ludwig von Mises Institute, Auburn, Alabama, 1995.

181. From a huge literature, see Jay H. Lehr, ed., *Rational Readings on Evironmental Concerns*, Van Nostrand Reinhold, New York, 1992; Ronald Bailye, *Eco-Scam: The False Prophets of Ecological Collapse*, St. Martin's Press, New York, 1993; Eric. W. Hagen & James W. Worman, *An Endless Series of Hobgoblins: The Science & Politics of Environmental Health Scares*, Foundation for Economic Education, Irvington on Hudson, New York, 1995

182. On the phenomenon of millenarianism see Norman Cohn, *The Pursuit of the Millennium: Revolutionary Messianism in Medieval and Reformation Europe and Its Bearing on Modern Totalitarianism*, Harper Torchbooks/Harper & Row, New York, 1961/Oxford University Press, 1970 and *Cosmos, Chaos, and the World to Come: The Ancient Roots of Apocalyptic Faith*, Yale University Press, 1993 and J. L. Talmon, *The Origins of Totalitarian Democracy*, Secker & Warburg, London, 1952 and *Political Messianism: The Romantic Phase*, Frederick A. Praeger, New York, 1962. Also see Eugene H. Methvin, *The Rise of Radicalism: The Social Psychology of Messianic Extremism*, Arlington House, New Rochelle, New York, 1973.

183. Pascal Bruckner, *The Tears of the White Man: Compassion As Contempt*, The Free Press, New York, 1986, pp. 68, 70-72, 75.

184. "Dry Facts and Follicles", *The Daily Telegraph*, 6 October, 1995.

185. *See Mary Douglas, Purity* and Danger: An Analysis of Concepts of Pollution and Taboo, Routledge and Kegan Paul, London, 1966; *Implicit Meanings*, Routledge and Kegan Paul, London, 1975; *Risk and Blame: Essays in Cultural Theory*, Routledge, London, 1992; and Idem & Aaron Wildavsky, *Risk and Culture: An Essay on the Selection of Technological and Environmental Dangers*, California University Press, 1982 and Risk

and Safety, University of California, Berkeley, 1982.

Aaron Wildavsky major 'solo' works on the subject are: "Richer Is Safer", *The Public Interest*, No. 60, Summer 1980; (1993), "Riskless Society", in Henderson, David, ed., *The Fortune Encyclopedia of Economics*, Warner Books, New York; *Trial Without Error: Anticipation vs Resilience as Strategies for Risk Reduction*, Centre for Independent Studies, St. Leonards, New South Wales, Occasional Paper No. 13, 1985; *Searching For Safety*, Social Philosophy & Policy Centre/Transaction Books, New Brunswick, New Jersey, 1988.

Also see Digby Anderson, "Why We Can't Have Safety Without Risk", *The Sunday Telegraph*, 27 August 1989; Paul Johnson, "The Perils of Risk Avoidance", *Regulation*, 4(3), May/June 1980, pp. 15-19; Ernest G. Ross, "The Two Faces of Risk", *The Freeman*, 33(12), December 1986, pp. 707-711; Malcolm Ross, "The Perils of Risk-Free Cancer Policy", *EPA Watch*, 4(5), 28 February 1995, pp. 4-6; Fred L. Smith, Jr., "Risks in the Modern World: What Prospects for Rationality?", *The Freeman*, 45(3), March 1995, pp. 140-144; John Adams, *Risk*, University College London Press, London, 1995.

186. Peter Berger, "Towards a Religion of Health Activism", in Idem et al, *Health, Lifestyle and Environment*, Social Affairs Unit/Manhattan Institute, London, 1991, p.25; Idem, "A Sociological View of the Antismoking Phenomenon", in Robert D. Tollison, ed., *Smoking & Society*, Op Cit, pp. 225-240. And see also Irving Kristol, "The Good Life and the New Class", in Berger, et al, *ibid*, pp. 146-152

187. Quoted in Robert Browning, "Who Are the Health Activists?" in *ibid*, p. 33.

188. Robert Matthews, "Cancer Reports Are 'Junk'", *The Sunday Correspondent*, 8 October, 1989.

189. James Le Fanu, *Environmental Alarums: A Medical Audit of Environmental Damage to Human Health*, Social Affairs Unit, London, 1994, p. 9. And see also P. H. Abelson, "Risk Assessments of Low-Level Exposures", Science, 265, 1994, p. 1507; Ben Bolch & Harold Lyons,"The Logic of the Toxic", Liberty, 8(1), November 1994, pp. 44-46, 67; Robert H. Nelson, "Chemicals and Witches: Standards of Evidence in Regulation", *The Freeman*, 45(3), March 1995, pp. 145-148 ; John R. Trotter, "Cancer: Incidental Exposures, Senescence or Both?", Ellsaessen, Hugh W., ed., Global 2000

Revisited: Mankind's Impact on Spaceship Earth, ICUS/Paragon House, New York, 1992, pp. 349-372

190. See Edith Efron, "The Big Cancer Lie", The American Spectator, 17(3), March 1984, pp. 10-17; "Behind the Cancer Terror", Reason, 4(9), 1984, pp. 17-18, and her magnum opus *The Apocalyptics: Cancer and the Big Lie*, Simon and Schuster, New York, 1984. Also notable is the work of Elizabeth Whelan. See *Toxic Terror*, Jameson Books, Ottawa, Ilinois, 1985/2nd edn. as *Toxic Terror: The Truth Behind the Cancer Scare*, Prometheus Books, Buffalo, New York, 1993; "Chemicals, Cancerphobia and Communication", Imprimis, 9(4), April 1980, pp. 1-5; "Cancer Scares And Our Inverted Health Priorities", Imprimis, 20(6), June 1991; "Malignant Cancer Scares", Regulation, 17(1), 1994, pp. 20-22 & Kathleen A. Meister, "Panic to the People", Reason, 14(1), May 1982, pp. 36- 40. Also see Bruce N. Ames, "Science and the Environment", The Freeman, 43(9), September 1993, pp. 343-344; *Does Curent Cancer Risk Assessment Harm Health?*, George C. Marshall Institute, Washington, D.C., 1994; et al eds., *What Are the Major Carcinogens in the Etiology of Human Cancer?: Important Advances in Oncology*, J. B. Lippincot, Philadelphia, 1989; & Lois Swirsky Gold "Cancer Prevemtion Strategies Greatly Exaggerate Risk", *Chemical & Engineering News*, January 1991; & Lois Swirsky Gold, "Natural Plant Pesticides Pose Greater Risks Than Synthetic Ones", *Chemical & Engineering News*, Jaunuary 1991; Lois Swirsky Gold, "Environmental Pollution and Cancer: Some Misconceptions", in Kenneth R. Foster, et al., eds., *Phantom Risk: Scientific Interference and the Law*, MIT Press, Cambridge, Mass., 1993; & Renae Magaw & Lois Swirsky Gold, "Ranking Possible Carcinogenic Hazards", *Science*, 236, 17 April 1991

191. See Roger J. Williams, "The Biology of Behaviour", *Saturday Review*, April 1971, also reprinted in Bettina B. Greaves, ed., *Free Market Economics: A Basic Reader*, Foundation for Economic Education, Irvington on Hudson, New York, 1975, pp. 10-14; "The Only Kind of People There Are", *The Freeman*, January 1969, reprinted in Bettina B. Greaves, ed., *Free Market Economics, op. cit.*, pp. 15-17; *Free and Unequal: The Biological Basis of Individual Liberty*, University of Texas Press, Austin, Texas, 1953/Liberty Press, Indianapolis, 1979; *Biochemical Individuality*,

John Wiley, New York, 1956; *You Are Extraordinary*, Random House, New York, 1967/Pyramid Books, New York, 1974

192. Petr Skrabanek, "Risk-Factor Epidemiology", in Berger et al, *op. cit.*, pp. 48-49. And see also Peter Lee, "The Need for Caution in Interpreting Low Level Risks Reported by Epidemiologists", in James Le Fanu, *Preventionitis: The Exaggerated Claims of Health Promotion*, Social Affairs Unit, London, 1994. And see "Editorial", "Testing for Carcinogens with Rodents", *Science*, 21 September, 1990, p. 1357, for an attack on "chemical witch-hunting". An earlier humorous attack on the orthodox approach was made in 1977 when Dr. George Moore of Denver General Hospital and Dr. William Palmer published a paper, "Money Causes Cancer: Ban It", in the *Journal of the American Cancer Society* in October 1977. In order to attack the "string of inane pronouncements" made by the Food and Drug Agency (FDA) and other "nonsense" by Federal decision-makers. They produced cancers by inserting sterilised 10 cent pieces into the peritoneal cavities in rats stomachs.

193. Skrabanek, *op. cit.*, p. 54

194. Peter D. Finch, "Creative Statistics", in *ibid*, pp. 81, 83, 86. For a longer discussion of the Lalonde Doctrine see Professor Peter D. Finch, "The 'Lalonde Doctrine' and Passive Smoking" and "Misleading Claims on Smoking and Health", *Policy* (Journal of the Centre For Independent Studies), Vol. 6, Nos. 2 and 3 respectively, reprinted in *Lies, Damned Lies ... A Close Look At the Statistics on Smoking and Health*, FOREST, London, 1991.

195. Karl R. Popper, *The Logic of Scientific Discovery* (1934), Routledge, London, 1992, pp. 280-281.

196. William Broad and Nicholas Wade, *Betrayers of the Truth*, Oxford University Press, Oxford, 1986, p. 36. See also Robert Bell, *Impure Science: Frauud, Compromise and Political Influence in Scientific Research*, John Wiley, New York, 1992 and Jean Rostand, *Error and Deception in Science*, Hutchinson, London, 1960; Paul R. Gross & Norman Levitt, *Higher Superstition: The Academic Left and Its Quarrels With Science*, Johns Hopkins University Press, 1994; Peter W. Huber, *Galileo's Revenge: Junk Science in The Courtroom*, Basic Books, New York, 1991

197. *ibid*, p. 181.

198. *ibid*, p. 223.

199. W. W. Bartley III, *Unfathomed Knowledge, Unmeasured*

Wealth: On Universties and the Wealth of Nations, Open Court, LaSalle, Illinois, 1990, pp. 94-164.
200. Beckmann, Op Cit, p. 3.
201. Peter Medawar, *The Limits of Science*, Oxford University Press, Oxford, 1985, p. 6.
202. Mark Mills, "Reactions to Health and Environmental Risks", in *ibid*, p. 105.
203. Vincent Marks, Is British Food Bad for You?, *op. cit.*, pp. 7-8.
204. Vincent Marks, "Exploding the Myths About Sugar", in Diet of Reason, *op. cit.*, p. 80.
205. In addition to the other SAU titles drawn upon in this paper see especially Petr Skrabanek, *The Death of Humane Medicine and the Rise of Coercive Healthism*, Social Affairs Unit, London, 1994. For other useful works see: Philip E. Ross, "Lies, Damned Lies & Medical Statistics", *Forbes*, August 1995; J. R. Johnstone & Chris Ulyatt, *Health Scare: The Misuse of Science in Public Health Policy*, Critical Issue No. 14, Australian Institute for Public Policy, Perth, 1991; Petr Skrabanek & James McCormick, *Follies and Fallacies in Medicine*, The Tarragon Press, Glasgow, 1989; ;Tom Holt, *The Rise of the Nanny State: How Consumer Advocates Try To Run Our Lives*, Capital Reserach Institute, Washington, DC, 1995; Thomas DiLorenzo, "The Crusade for Politically Correct Consumption", *The Freeman*, 45(9), September 1995, pp. 557-560; Fabian Tassano, *The Power of Life and Death: A Critique of Medical Tyranny*, Duckworth, London, 1995; Jacob Sullum, "What the Doctor Orders", *Reason,* 27(8), January 1996, pp. 20-27; Cynthia Crosses, *Tainted Truth: The Manipulation of Fact in America*, Simon & Schuster, New York, 1995; Nicholas Everstadt, *The Tyranny of Numbers: Mismeasure and Misrule*, American Enterprise Institute, Washington, DC, 1995; John Allens, John Allen, *A Mathematician Reads the Newspapers*, Basic Books, New York, 1995; William W. Van Alstyne, *A New Free Speech Problem: Government Propaganda Against Business*, Legal Backgrounder 5-27, Washington Legal Foundation, Washington, 1990; James T. Bennett, & Thomas J. DiLorenzo, *Official Lies: How Washington Misleads Us*, Groom Books, Alexandria, Virginia, 1992; Richard T. Kaplar, Richard T. & Patrick D. Maines, Patrick D., *The Government Factor: Undermining Journalistic Ethics in the Information Age*,

1995; Daniel D. Polsby, Daniel D., *A Case of Official Political Correctness: Anti-Industry Propaganda*, Legal Backgrounder, Washington Legal Foundation, Washington, DC, 1991; John Semmens, "Public Policy Debate: The Rigged Game", The Freeman, 38(10),October 1998, pp. 395-397.

206 "Letters", *The Times*, 3 June 1992, p. 15.

207. *Ad-Issues*, January 1995, p. 2.

208. For various critical perspectives on determinism see Dennis H. Wrong, "Human Nature and the Perspective of Sociology", *Social Research*, Vol. 30, No. 3, Autumn 1963; Idem, "The Oversocialized Conception of Man in Modern Sociology", *American Sociological Review*, Vol. 26, No. 2, April 1961; Benjamin Schwartz, "The Socio-Historic Approach", *World Politics*, Vol. VIII, No. 1, October 1955; Murray N. Rothbard, "The Mantle of Science", in H. Schoeck and J. W. Wiggins, eds., *Scientism and Values*, Van Nostrand, Princeton, New Jersey, 1960; Keith Dixon, *The Sociology of Belief: Fallacy and Foundation*, Routledge and Kegan Paul, London, 1980; Tibor Machan, *The Pseudo-Science of B. F. Skinner*, Arlington House, New Rochelle, New York, 1974 Antony Flew, *Thinking About Social Thinking*, Basil Blackwell, Oxford, 1985; Idem, *A Rational Animal*, Oxford University, 1978; Idem, "Metaphysical Idealism and the Sociology of Knowledge", in *Sociology, Equality and Education*, Macmillan, London, 1976; Kenneth Minogue, "The Myth of Social Conditioning", *Policy Review*, No. 18, Fall 1981; Martin Hollis, *Models of Man: Philosophic Thoughts on Social Action*, Cambridge University Press, 1977; Richard Taylor, *Action and Purpose*, Prentice-Hall, Englewood Cliffs, New Jersey, 1966; Rom Harre and P. F. Secord, *The Explanation of Social Behaviour*, Basil Blackwell, Oxford, 1972; Nathanel Branden, *The Psychology of Self-Esteem*, Nash Publishing, Los Angeles, 1969; Wallace I. Matson, *Sentience*, California University Press, 1977; Michael Polanyi, *Personal Knowledge: Towards A Post-Critical Philosophy*, Routledge and Kegan Paul, London, 1951; Idem, *The Study of Man*, Routledge and Kegan Paul, London, 1959; Ludwig von Bertalanfy, *Robots, Men and Mind*, George Braziller, New York, 1967; Joseph Agassi, *Towards a Rational Philosophical Anthropology*, Martinus Nijhoff, The Hague, Amsterdam, 1977; Arthur Koestler and J. R. Smythies, eds., *Beyond Reductionism*, Hutchinson, London, 1969; Abraham Maslow, *Toward A Psychology of Being*, 2nd edn., D. Van

Nostrand, Princeton, New Jersey, 1968; Edmund Ions, *Against Behaviouralism*, Basil Blackwell, Oxford, 1977. Chris Tame has also dealt with the question in "Change and Pseudo-Change in Sociology", *The Jewish Journal of Sociology*, Vol. XIX, No. 1, June 1977 and "The New Enlightenment", in *The 'New Right' Enlightenment*, Economic and Literary Books, Sevenoaks, Kent, 1985.

209. Minette Marin, "Signs of the Times", *The Sunday Telegraph*, 6 February 1994.

End Matters

Many thanks for buying this book. Many thanks for reading it. Sales of my books are useful to my finances, and they help assure me that I have not been typing away without hope of influence and fame. If you liked it, please consider leaving a review on your local Amazon. Reviews are very important for further sales. Even if you disagree with what I have said, please go ahead and review the book.

You may also wish to look up some of my other books on Amazon. There are many of these. Under my own name, Sean Gabb, I write both non-fiction and fiction. Under the pen-name, Richard Blake, I am writing a long series of historical novels set in the early Byzantine Empire. There are now twelve of these, and they have been commercially translated into half a dozen languages. Though not overtly political, they do manage to reflect my general view of life, and may be of interest. I might add that, in hard copy, they make interesting presents for those hard-to-please loved ones!

Otherwise, please feel free to connect with me on Facebook and on various other social media platforms. Or feel free to contact me directly—sean@seangabb.co.uk or via my websites:

https://www.seangabb.co.uk/
http://www.richardblake.me.uk/
http://www.classicstuition.co.uk/

Best regards,

Sean Gabb
Deal

Printed in Poland
by Amazon Fulfillment
Poland Sp. z o.o., Wrocław

54354407R00090